DATA
ANALYTICS

A Road Map for Expanding
Analytics Capabilities

DATA
ANALYTICS

A Road Map for Expanding
Analytics Capabilities

Richard Cline
Ward Melhuish, CSSGB
Meredith Murphy, CFE, CAMS

The IIA's International Professional Practices Framework (IPPF) comprises the full range of existing and developing practice guidance for the profession. The IPPF provides guidance to internal auditors globally and paves the way to world-class internal auditing.

The IIA and the Foundation work in partnership with researchers from around the globe who conduct valuable studies on critical issues affecting today's business world. Much of the content presented in their final reports is a result of Foundation-funded research and prepared as a service to the Foundation and the internal audit profession. Expressed opinions, interpretations, or points of view represent a consensus of the researchers and do not necessarily reflect or represent the official position or policies of The IIA or the Foundation.

"Grant Thornton" refers to Grant Thornton LLP, the U.S. member firm of Grant Thornton International Ltd (GTIL), and/or refers to the brand under which the GTIL members firms provide audit, tax, and advisory services to their clients, as the context requires. GTIL and each of its member firms are separate legal entities and are not a worldwide partnership. GTIL does not provide services to clients. Services are delivered by the member firms in their respective countries. GTIL and its member firms are not agents of, and do not obligate, one another and are not liable for one another's acts or omissions. In the United States, visit grantthornton.com for details.

ISBN-13: 978-1-63454-022-3
22 21 20 19 18   1 2 3 4 5 6

Printed in Canada

CONTENTS

LIST OF EXHIBITS

FOREWORD

The accelerating pace of technological advancement and increasing volumes of data has resulted in data analytics and innovation being a top priority for organizations and internal audit departments. The strategy for integrating analytics into an organization, or department, has the ability to transform how a company operates, innovates, and evolves. This book is intended to help companies develop their road map for expanding analytics capabilities.

The daily operations at most companies are ripe with opportunities to streamline and improve functions and processes, and data analytics holds the key to unlocking these opportunities. As such, chief audit executives and internal auditors have the potential to add value to their organizations in more ways than ever before—as long as they understand the power they wield and the potential of data analytics to add value and set them apart from competitors.

The Institute of Internal Auditors (IIA) partnered with Grant Thornton to conduct research and provide subject matter expertise to shed light on the ever-changing uses of data analytics and how companies and internal auditors can—and do—harness analytics.

We hope you will use this road map for expanding analytics capabilities as you pursue data analytics, innovate, and tackle your digital transformation. Ultimately, we want you to increase the value of your data, become more efficient, better assess and avoid risk, and capture the new (and often unexpected) benefits of analytics.

| Richard Cline | Ward Melhuish | Meredith Murphy |

ACKNOWLEDGMENTS

The Internal Audit Foundation would like to thank the Board of Trustees, the Committee of Research and Education Advisors (CREA) members, and staff for dedicating their talent and expertise to the project.

James Alexander, CREA Member

Steve Mar, CREA Member

Tania Stegemann, CREA Member

Lee Ann Campbell, Managing Editor, Internal Audit Foundation

Candace Sacher, Product Manager, Internal Audit Foundation

Eva Sweet, Director, Global Standards & Guidance, The IIA

No one person could possibly have tackled the research, planning, drafting, editing, and compiling of insights required to create this book. The IIA and Grant Thornton are grateful to the individuals and companies that participated in the research and surveys that led to many of the insights in this book.

We would also like to thank the following organizations and individuals for sharing their insights into how data analytics can maximize value for companies and the internal audit community.

Barbican
Faisal Butt, Group Head of Internal Audit

BBA Aviation
Basil Dixon, Senior Manager of Internal Audit

BNP Paribas
Andrew Hall, Head of Data Fabric

Cargill
Laurence Uzureau, Director of Internal Audit

CF Industries
Mary Ann Tourney, Vice President (CAE), Internal Audit

Chevron Services Company
Angelina Butler, Audit Manager
Linda Ware, Senior Auditor

Cleveland Clinic
Don Sinko, Chief Integrity Officer

Coca-Cola European Partners
Anthony Dench, Associate Director of IT Audit

Deutsche Bank
Mayur Halai, Vice President of Internal Audit

Diageo
Ana Acuna, Global Audit & Risk Strategy Director

Fifth Third Bancorp
Pat Cappel, Senior Business and Predictive Analytics Manager, Audit Division

FSCS
Nicola Wood, Head of Internal Audit

G4S
Trevor Gelnar, Group Director Risk & Internal Audit

Howdens Joinery Co
Zoe Williams, Head of Internal Audit & Risk

Acknowledgments

KeyBank
Greg Steffine, SVP and Director, Business Intelligence & Analytics Competency Center

Lloyds Banking Group
Shehryar Humayun, Head of Audit - Data Analytics

Meggitt
Simon Richardson, Group Head of Audit & Risk

Miller
Prashant Amatya, Head of Audit

MoneyGram
Manny Rosenfeld, Senior Vice President of Internal Audit

OZ Management
Michael Rosenberg, Chief Audit Executive, Vice President Internal Audit

Royal Bank of Scotland
Martin Ambrose, Head of Audit

Shop Direct
Peter Johnson, Head of Audit & Investment Finance

Smith & Nephew
David Lynam, Director of Internal Audit

Sprint
Karen Begelfer, Vice President, Corporate Audit Services
Brady Rothrock, Data Scientist

The Co-operative Bank plc
Tim Frost, Head of Audit – IT, Change & Third Parties

Visa

Ibrahim Motiwala, Director, Internal Controls, Controllership

Wates Group

Simon Rose, Group Head of Internal Audit

Whitbread PLC

Jags Mann, Group Head of IT Audit

The professionals of Grant Thornton LLP dedicated considerable resources to write a book that would benefit organizations, executives, and the broader internal audit community. We make special acknowledgment of the following individuals.

Name	Title	Location
Chris Bell	Principal	Houston, TX
Mike Briggs	Director	Los Angeles, CA
Vishal Chawla	Principal	Arlington, VA
Bryan Doyle	Senior Associate	Chicago, IL
Tom Estella	Director	Atlanta, GA
Arri Hoyland	Manager	Minneapolis, MN
Alex Hunt	Director	United Kingdom
Bailey Jordan	Partner	Raleigh, NC
Alex Koltsov	Manager	Phoenix, AZ
Rich Lanza	Director	Iselin, NJ
Tracy Maddaloni	Manager	Appleton, WI
Lester McHargue	Director	Atlanta, GA
Jamie O'Riordan	Director	Boston, MA
Bruce Orr	Director	Houston, TX
Brad Preber	Partner	Phoenix, AZ
Ethan Rojhani	Partner	Denver, CO

Name	Title	Location
Mike Rose	Partner	Philadelphia, PA
Priya Sarjoo	Principal	Dallas, TX
Srikant Sastry	Principal	Alexandria, VA
Shawn Stewart	Partner	Irvine, CA
Warren Stippich	Partner	Chicago, IL

We would also like to thank the editorial team at Leff Communications who worked closely with Grant Thornton to bring together the subject matter expertise, research, and insights collected during the one-on-one interviews with chief audit executives, internal audit directors, and data analytics leaders.

ABOUT THE AUTHORS

Richard Cline is the managing director of data analytics at Grant Thornton. He has 35 years of management and technology consulting experience and specializes in technology transformation, systems implementation, and analytics solutions. Before joining Grant Thornton, Richard spent 13 years at IBM, five of which he devoted to leading the North America Oracle practice. He was also a partner in PricewaterhouseCoopers LLP's management consulting series group and has extensive experience with programs that optimize and monetize a wide variety of digital and physical assets. He has particular expertise in business case and return on investment development for IoT projects, digital manufacturing, predictive maintenance and optimization, and after-market and warranty optimization. He holds a degree in business administration and information systems from the Haslam College of Business at the University of Tennessee.

Ward Melhuish, CSSGB, is a principal with Grant Thornton LLP where he serves as the advisory leader for the firm's consumer and industrial products industry team as well as the advisory services leader for data analytics. He has more than 30 years of experience and specializes in performance improvement and transformation services ranging from strategy development and deployment to cost assessment and analytics. Ward has worked with commercial and government clients across numerous industries, including financial services, industrial operations, manufacturing, logistics, law enforcement and security, and electric power generation. He is a former Naval Officer and holds a bachelor of science in aerospace engineering from the University of Virginia and an MBA from Loyola University.

Meredith Murphy, CFE, CAMS, is a director within Grant Thornton's Data Analytics Center of Excellence. She has spent more than 16 years helping clients create value, protect value, and transform. Her primary areas of focus are developing and executing growth strategies, enabling clients with analytic insights, and providing forensic and investigative expertise. Prior to Grant Thornton LLP, Meredith created value for clients within the forensic practice of PricewaterhouseCoopers LLP. She holds an MBA from the W.P. Carey School of Business at Arizona State University, is a Certified Fraud Examiner (CFE), a Certified Anti-Money Laundering Specialist (CAMS), and has been trained and certified in change management methodologies.

INTRODUCTION

With every technological innovation or business breakthrough, executives naturally ask, "What does it mean for my company?" and, "How can we incorporate it to create value or gain a competitive advantage?" The accelerating pace of technological advancement means that these questions are being asked with increasing volume and frequency.

Over the past few years, use of data to enable analytics insight has become a top priority for organizations. In *Data Analytics: Elevating Internal Audit's Value*, published in 2016 in partnership with the Internal Audit Foundation, we sought to provide internal auditors with a base of knowledge to assess the analytics maturity of their organization as a first step in building capabilities. Since then, companies have integrated analytics into functions across their enterprises, particularly to support sales and marketing efforts.

Analytics applications have the potential to transform how internal audit operates and enhance the value delivered to the organization. As a back-office function, using analytics to support internal audit may not be a priority for many companies, even though the integrity and confidence in corporate financial data forms the basis for most management decisions and improvement initiatives. There's also the question of how internal audit functions must adapt to embrace the capabilities of the technology—and the additional skills and expertise they will need to acquire to harness the full potential of analytics.

This book was written to help chief audit executives (CAEs) and the internal audit function create a road map for expanding analytic capabilities, and to help make a case for investing in analytics. Since companies run the gamut in their awareness and ability to embrace analytics and embark on an analytics-driven transformation, we sought to address the broadest possible audience.

Accordingly, the first several chapters provide an overview of the critical elements of an analytics effort, discuss a framework for digital transformation, and cover how to identify the highest-value priorities. The last three chapters discuss specific applications of analytics in internal audit and offer detailed examples.

Every company has unique strengths and capabilities, so the starting point for an analytics effort will vary accordingly. While success will require a sustained commitment as well as flexibility to adapt to emerging technologies and new innovations, the insights in this book offer readers specific actions they can pursue to position their organization—and internal audit specifically—to unlock the full potential of data and analytics.

Chapter

1

THE KEYS TO ANALYTICS SUCCESS

"A point of view can be a dangerous luxury when substituted for insight and understanding."

—Marshall McLuhan

For centuries, business leaders relied primarily on intellect, acumen, experience, and gut instinct to make difficult decisions. Over the past several decades, however, digital technologies, analytics, and data-driven insights have ushered in an era of more information that supports better decision making and better results. Tech milestones, such as Deep Blue's defeat of chess champion Garry Kasparov and Google AlphaGo's victory over human players in the game Go, illustrate the advancement and dominance of computers and analytics.[1]

The divergent fortunes of experts and machines also highlight an interesting contradiction: before we began to rely so heavily on technology, a company's experts fueled its growth. More recently, technology is increasingly in the spotlight, often overshadowing human talent. This development has sometimes led companies to treat technology as if it were a silver bullet.

Analytics driven by technology and capabilities can be impressive, but this isn't a road show. It is your business. Data hold insight, but it is people—not data—who ensure that analytics generate value for the company. It is leadership's responsibility to drive the collection of insights, increase understanding of processes and opportunities for improvement, and create value for the organization and its customers.

As talk about innovation and disruption permeates strategy meetings and executive priorities, analytics and digitization are becoming critical elements of vision statements and core business objectives. Advances in technology are raising expectations, creating new needs, and transforming the way business is done—and the way we aspire to do business.

To unleash the potential of such advances, leaders must anticipate the needs of their company and customers, invest in innovation, and deploy resources that are focused on results to effectively generate the highest return on those investments. Analytics and digitization remain on the innovation agenda because of their potential to create value and improve insights (see exhibit 1-1).

Companies know the importance of embedding analytics into every level of their organization. In fact, 92 percent of senior leaders understand the value of integrating enterprisewide data analytics.[2] But leaders at all levels struggle to maximize the return on their investment—66 percent indicated that the internal audit department has a sponsor and/or organizational structure that allows for an effective analytics function within the department.[3] Surprisingly, though, when looking across the enterprise, only 25 percent of survey respondents felt that their company was structured appropriately to support an effective analytics program. Sponsorship and the right organizational structure play a vital role—and can make or break an analytics program.

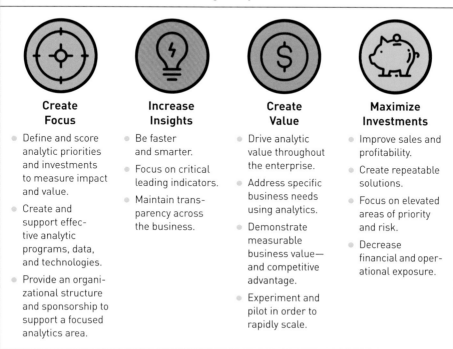

Exhibit 1-1: Analytics Continue to Be a Core Desired Competency for Organizations and Leaders, Offering Many Benefits

Create Focus	Increase Insights	Create Value	Maximize Investments
• Define and score analytic priorities and investments to measure impact and value.	• Be faster and smarter.	• Drive analytic value throughout the enterprise.	• Improve sales and profitability.
• Create and support effective analytic programs, data, and technologies.	• Focus on critical leading indicators.	• Address specific business needs using analytics.	• Create repeatable solutions.
• Provide an organizational structure and sponsorship to support a focused analytics area.	• Maintain transparency across the business.	• Demonstrate measurable business value—and competitive advantage.	• Focus on elevated areas of priority and risk.
		• Experiment and pilot in order to rapidly scale.	• Decrease financial and operational exposure.

Source: ◉ GrantThornton

The Role of Sponsorship

From Little League baseball diamonds to Major League Baseball's commanding stadiums, individuals and teams rely on astute managers to direct their efforts in a way that can ensure success. As in baseball, some of the best leaders in business have been visionaries, master tacticians, and brilliant motivators. Similarly, the best teams have enjoyed consistent support from a sponsor (senior management or executive) who dedicated time, money, and resources to maximize the team or organization's opportunities for success.

Without adequate sponsorship, individuals and teams can lack sufficient resources or direction, forcing them to adopt a reactive stance to decision making and strategy. Sponsorship—championing an initiative, providing direction and strategy, or ensuring the sufficient allocation of resources—for an analytics program is not a spectator sport. Effective sponsorship requires collaboration and agreement across an organization to enable consistent governance, prioritization of opportunities, and resource allocation. Achieving the desired balance across an enterprise requires regular collaboration; timely decision making at both a strategic and tactical level; and an environment in which teams are allowed to drive rapid innovation, experiment, and fail fast.

Sponsorship for analytics exists across the largest companies and leadership agendas. In a recent study conducted by Grant Thornton, 44 percent of respondents—primarily CAEs—reported that analytics was one of their "principal professional responsibilities." In addition to CAEs, chief executives continue to tout the importance of data analytics on leadership agendas.

Our recent survey highlights a dichotomy: while sponsorship for analytics exists in companies, less than 40 percent of respondents reported that their organization consistently uses analytics (see exhibit 1-2).[4]

Exhibit 1-2: Most Companies Are Not Consistently Using Analytics

To what extent does your organization use data analytics?

<40% CONSISTENTLY LEVERAGE ANALYTICS

Source: Grant Thornton

For those who do use data analytics, the surveys indicate that the majority of organizations are using analytics to diagnose operational and business situations and problems. For example, CAEs use analytics most commonly for compliance testing and forensic analysis. But if companies had adequate sponsorship and resources, they would be poised to improve decision making through continuous monitoring, continuous auditing, predictive analytics, and machine learning. Such tools would enable them to focus on risk areas they have previously overlooked. For example, the survey reveals that respondents are least likely to say their organization uses analytics to manage cybersecurity risks, even though cyber attacks and security breaches have become an increasing threat in recent years (see exhibit 1-3).

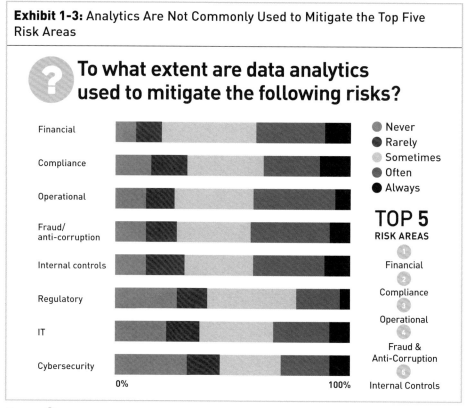

Exhibit 1-3: Analytics Are Not Commonly Used to Mitigate the Top Five Risk Areas

Source: Grant Thornton

For individuals who sponsor or are involved with an analytics program, the following recommendations can help make this initiative more successful.

Create a Forward-Looking Vision and Engage Leaders Across the Enterprise to Align Aspirations and Needs

When teams clearly understand the company's vision and goals, they can align their individual goals with those of the enterprise. Executives and subject-matter experts (SMEs) are responsible for determining how a company uses analytics, so a vision for how a company needs to transform through analytics must be a common aspiration of leaders across the organization. Once an aspirational vision has been created (for more on developing a vision, see chapter 4), executives and managers must commit to share and reinforce it on a continual basis. (See sidebar, "Promoting Digitization Throughout the Enterprise.") Your team will internalize this vision and embody it around their colleagues, ensuring that the vision becomes infused into the company's culture.

While the vision will vary depending on a person's role or business objectives, the underlying tenets remain the same. Our interviews find that CEOs have a desire to gain strategic insights, whereas business unit leaders are more focused on analytics tools and capabilities to provide tactical and operational insights and efficiencies. It is critical to align aspirations and needs when making investments in analytics. CAEs and internal audit directors described the following analytics needs:

- Predictive modeling capabilities
- Benchmarking capabilities
- Risk-based monitoring
- Analytics to refine scoping on audit jobs
- Resources to stay on top of innovation changes in the industry and analytics
- How to leverage analytics to identify new and emerging risks

> ## Promoting Digitization Throughout the Enterprise
>
> Digitization is often a necessary prerequisite to integrating analytics into operations. A large private company's executive team believed that digitization, coupled with an analytics effort, was critical to the company's business strategy and growth. To promote digitization, team members sought to incorporate it into every employee's career development. Executives and business leaders described it as a desired capability and launched a challenge to reinforce digitization as a priority. The challenge consisted of three components: a live exhibition that described the capabilities and allowed employees to "touch" and "feel" a variety of digitization concepts; online training on digitization and new tools; and a platform that allowed employees to share knowledge, present innovative ideas, and be recognized for their contributions. These ongoing efforts helped the company create and promote a digital culture.

Involve Executives and Influencers to Enhance Sponsorship

A recent McKinsey global survey reported that the "most significant reason for organizations' effectiveness at data and analytics" is "ensuring senior-management involvement in data and analytics activities."[5] Our interviews corroborate that the involvement of senior management enhances sponsorship and therefore improves the success of analytics programs.

Focus on Leadership

Employees are the key to success. Sponsors are responsible for ensuring that their company has the necessary talent to manage the integration and execution of analytics. Depending on the analytics program structure, the sponsor may be the chief financial officer (CFO), chief information officer (CIO), chief accounting officer (CAO), or another leader. Don't overlook the importance of people—in particular, sponsorship and a commitment to resources.

Build a Change Management Plan into the Process

In many organizations, aversion to change is the largest inhibitor to growth and innovation. In addition to standard resistance factors, when analytics resources are being centrally led, people across the business can be skeptical of the ecosystem and data over which they do not have control. It is critical for leaders to acknowledge the disruption that analytics and innovation will cause and incorporate an organizational change-management plan into their efforts.

Organizational Structure as a Key to Success

Within the companies we interviewed, the organizational structures, maturity of analytics programs, company sizes, and industries varied significantly. While most companies aspire to have a central analytics function that supports the organization (a Center of Excellence), the leadership styles and operating models they employ often inhibit successful adoption in these hub-and-spoke organizations. Here are some ways to support a successful organizational structure.

Create Collaboration, Not Segregation

While it is appealing to have a centralized function to handle all analytics requests from business units, the business cannot simply give orders to an IT employee or data scientist and expect a positive outcome. Successful analytics efforts require the collaboration of data experts and employees with the requisite business and industry acumen. For example, a company might create a Center of Excellence (CoE) or analytics council that would include a representative (or sponsor) from each of the business units. The CoE or council would then meet regularly (anywhere from daily to quarterly, depending on the organization and its analytics initiatives) to remain aligned on vision, needs, priorities, and allocation of resources. This model gives each business unit a resource in the council to represent its needs and further inform the analytics efforts.

Prioritize and Stay Focused

Once business units become aware of the benefits of an analytics team, the analytics employees can become overwhelmed by demands on their time. One company told us that more than 50 percent of its analytics requests came from business units whose projects were not related to the overarching business strategy and priorities. To be successful, teams must track requests, align to the company's overall vision and priorities, and stay focused.

Ensure Alignment with the IT Department

Internal audit and other teams working with analytics often struggle to manage enterprise resource planning (ERP) changes and evolving data. For example, one interviewee noted that unexpected changes to the IT architecture and underlying data altered historical records and reduced the completeness and accuracy of reporting insights without the company's knowledge. The changes had an adverse impact on the company's reports. These issues are caused by poor change-management practices and IT and data governance, as changes must be approved by the business after gaining an understanding of the possible impacts. To create alignment with the IT department, an organization's operating model must allow transparency into two areas. First, executives should understand the major applications within their IT environment and how they fit into the analytics program. Second, the evolving IT landscape means that executives must remain connected so that the company's technology platform can adapt to the IT environment and data changes.

Build an Analytics Bench

Every company has a different strategy for building out its analytics team. However, our interviews and surveys revealed companies are looking for many of the same characteristics and capabilities, including the following:

- Analytics experience during university studies or appliece—the ability to build queries and match and merge files

- The IT, data, and computer science capabilities needed to move into advanced analytics

- Critical-thinking skills

- Visualization skills (e.g., Microsoft Power BI, Tableau)

- An inquisitive nature

- Confidence (specifically, candidates who aren't threatened by what they don't know)

- Self-motivation to accomplish and drive change

But developing and acquiring this talent is a challenge. In fact, 54 percent of internal audit professionals surveyed find it moderately, very, or extremely challenging to maintain the in-house expertise necessary to staff a data analytics team; 62 percent find it moderately, very, or extremely challenging to recruit talent.[6] So what do they do? Depending on their analytics resources, companies build analytics capabilities in a variety of ways. While some organizations hire PhDs or data scientists, others develop existing talent by sending employees to data-science programs; enrolling them in online courses, such as through HarvardX or Coursera; or getting them involved in technology groups with local organizations. Others are exploring partnerships or acquisitions in an effort to ramp up their analytics capabilities more quickly. All such efforts can help organizations build well-rounded teams that can support the effective use and implementation of analytics.

Once executives understand their role in leading an analytics program, they're ready to integrate analytics throughout their organization. This book provides a road map to that process, with insights for each step of the way:

- A primer on analytics, including recent trends and developments and a look at how companies are using analytics to increase revenues and generate value

- A discussion of digital transformation as a key enabler of analytics

- A framework for assessing and prioritizing the use cases for analytics that will provide the most value to the organization

- A guide for how to identify, aggregate, and analyze the right data for the selected use cases

- A proven approach for measuring the return on investment (ROI) of analytics efforts

- An approach to using analytics to support enterprise risk management (ERM) and risk assessments

Whether your company is just starting down the path or is well versed in analytics, this material will help you take your strategy to the next level. Continued innovation and technological advances are creating new applications for these technologies. It will be up to executives to strike the optimal balance between humans and machines and unlock the full potential of analytics in their organization.

Chapter

2

THE CHANGING DATA AND ANALYTICS NEEDS OF COMPANIES

"I do not believe you can do today's job with yesterday's methods and be in business tomorrow."

—NELSON JACKSON

The rapid evolution of uses of data and analytics is creating challenges for companies. Executives broadly understand the need to invest in analytics, but they don't have access to the data they need, don't know how to use it, and don't know how it fits into their risk profile and strategy. This chapter offers a brief overview of different analytics techniques (including artificial intelligence and machine learning) and how companies are deploying these analytics today to increase revenues and profitability. Specific use cases highlight the strategic and operational benefits that companies can achieve through data and analytics.

The Data Imperative: Moving Beyond the 3Vs

In the not-too-distant past, data and analytics were a much more modest under-taking. As recently as the 1990s, information was seen as data that existed in rows and columns. Additionally, older systems could only export data in a simple format in which all the data elements in a record were separated by commas and all the data were structured. Organizations would merge two of these big, flat files—say, one of customers and another of transactions—to analyze each of these segments and look for correlations between customer information and their associated transactions. A large customer file might comprise three to five million rows.

Companies would typically use these customer files as "push files" to analyze behaviors. This process was the standard—and it was cumbersome and time-consuming. But it helped lay the foundation for a future work environment in which business strategies and decisions rely heavily on analytical thinking and data analysis. These beginnings made it possible for organizations to continue to invest in data storage, analytical tools, and the like—all of which have become more and more critical to business functions.

The volume, velocity, and variety of data (the 3Vs) have all increased exponentially over the past decade. Beginning around 2005, the 3Vs changed significantly, and the available value from that data scaled with it. In 2002, for example, we worked with a top-three U.S. bank whose 13-terabyte database for its mortgage business was one of the largest customer databases in banking at the time. We now live in a world in which Facebook reportedly creates four petabytes—4,000 terabytes—of data *each day*. This volume of information enables everything from customer segmentation and product suggestions on retail websites to more effective health diagnoses—not just for groups of people, but also on an individual basis.

To process these massive amounts of data, new data-management processes needed to be implemented. While businesses committed to redesigning their processes and building new capabilities, the 3Vs continued to expand at an ever faster pace. Decision makers wanted quicker answers based on more data and refused to accept analyses of data that were months, or even weeks, old. The world moved to 24-hour news cycles and instantaneous social-media reporting, and most people have come to expect up-to-date answers and immediate access to information.

Through all of this change, the mathematical procedures used to analyze data stayed constant; they were just applied to different types of problems, and, over time, they were used to process huge amounts of data to get answers. But today, companies need to take a different approach to data storage and management in order for data to support their business goals. We have all heard that "storage is cheap." However, the new data sources are so massive that companies must filter and aggregate data as they are created and store only the pertinent information in warehouses to have any hope of producing meaningful insights quickly. Surprisingly, 66 percent of internal audit professionals report that their company has no plans or specific timing for upgrading their data analytics tools.[1]

A few tools in the marketplace can aggregate data, but most require human intervention to be effective. Companies must identify which parts of the data are important so they can calibrate the aggregation tools. If a company makes a mistake during this step, it will lose critical information and waste money on storing worthless information. Leading this task can be difficult; it takes an experienced data scientist with subject-matter expertise to build the appropriate analytical model.

Data and Analytics: Techniques and Technologies

Once companies have identified and gathered the relevant data, there are many methods they can use to extract insight and value from this information. Analytics processes vary widely based on the data that information analysts are looking for, how they intend to use it, and their understanding of technology and the industry. For a CAE, the pairing of a risk-based approach with relevant data and analytics can create focus, resource efficiencies, and value.

Techniques

Data analysts are likely to focus on four types of analytics: descriptive, diagnostic, predictive, and prescriptive (in order of increasing sophistication and complexity). The use of each type is determined by the task at hand and how the insights will be used.[2]

Descriptive analytics is the least sophisticated and most frequently used analytics technique as it requires little synthesis or analysis. Analysts use this method to report and characterize past events by condensing large chunks of data into smaller, more meaningful bits of information.

Diagnostic analytics provides insight into why certain trends or specific incidents occurred. Analysts using diagnostic analytics can evaluate data in different and deeper ways—for example, by segmenting by product, region, or customer—and therefore gain a better understanding of business performance, market dynamics, and the impact of different inputs on outcome.

Predictive analytics allows users to identify trends and forecast outcomes by extracting information from large volumes of existing data, applying certain assumptions, and drawing correlations.

Prescriptive analytics requires a significant volume of data to link predictions to actions that will produce the best result. If predictive analytics seeks to determine demand, prescriptive analytics answers the question, "How do I align my business to maximize profit if demand is X?"

Internal auditors today use descriptive, and sometimes diagnostic, analytics to decipher the atmosphere and analyze where errors have occurred. But businesses and their internal audit functions are increasingly turning to predictive and prescriptive analytics.

Technologies

Despite these consistent, basic approaches to analytics, the tools and technologies that analysts use to derive insights are changing constantly, allowing for better and more efficient analysis. Two recent additions to the toolkit are artificial intelligence and machine learning.

Artificial Intelligence

Artificial intelligence (AI) is the development of computer systems able to perform tasks that normally require human intelligence, such as visual perception, speech recognition, and decision making. As an analytics tool, AI gives companies the ability to see specific new patterns in data, almost in real time. Through AI, analysts can create a process that sets parameters for a modeling structure and uses logical steps to recreate the model in real time based on recent historical data (for example, from earlier that day).

AI is already present in our everyday lives, and our reliance on AI-enabled features is growing. When you ask Siri or Alexa a question, an answer is generated by AI. Autonomous vehicles are another example of AI applications, harnessing huge amounts of data to navigate streets and recognize other cars and pedestrians. Companies such as Narrative Science, which uses AI to generate written articles (say, a recap for a college football game) based on information (game statistics), are starting to blur the line between machines and what was once perceived as the unassailable domain of humans. The coming years will see the integration of AI applications into daily life and business processes at an accelerating pace.

Machine Learning

An IA application, machine learning provides systems with the ability to automatically learn and improve from experience without being explicitly programmed. Machine learning focuses on the development of computer programs that can access data and then use those data to learn for themselves.

In the past, analysts built algorithms that could predict who was likely to respond, purchase, or complete a specific action based on historical data. Using data from the previous six months, they could find trends and patterns. They could then use the algorithm to "score" current data—say, once per week—to tag the company's highest prospects. This list of prospects could be used in applications such as direct marketing. This method was valuable, but new trends in the marketplace could only be identified when the algorithm was updated, which might happen only twice a year.

Today, analysts can construct algorithms that create new algorithms within themselves, enabling them to rebuild and refocus continually. Every Sunday morning, for instance, the machine can gather the available information, search for new patterns and trends, and score the entire population on the most recent model, which has information available and entered from the previous day.

Enabling an algorithm to work this way and removing the human component of algorithm creation can cause issues. Machines can easily make models, but they don't always understand the business application of the models. For this reason, the analytics operation must be overseen by a collaborative team of data scientists, strategists, and stakeholders. The data scientist will understand the mathematics, while others on the team can ensure that their work meets business objectives.

How Data and Analytics Can Increase Revenues and Profitability

Every company generates huge amounts of data from customer transactions, equipment and sensors, internal operations, online traffic, social media, and other sources. The question for executives is how to harness the data and apply the right analytics methods to create business value. The answer varies not just by company and industry but also by the volumes and types of data available to an organization. Following are just a few of the ways in which companies are using data and analytics to unleash value.

Create Business Models and Revenue Streams

Companies that naturally find themselves at the intersection of huge amounts of data traffic are in an enviable position to launch businesses that generate their value from data and analytics. Just as drugs developed for one purpose can be applied effectively to treat other conditions—such as Botox being used to treat migraine headaches—companies can launch new ventures or acquire and modify existing businesses based on their access to data. For example, when Google acquired YouTube, the latter was primarily a video-sharing platform. Now it has become the second-most-popular search engine (after Google), a content-delivery platform with algorithms that support video recommendations, a content engine, and a huge revenue generator. Meanwhile, GE has embarked on a journey to transform its business model from a manufacturer of industrial machines to a data company. From jet engines to locomotives to heavy machinery, GE's equipment has sensors that produce more and more data, leading the company to invest billions in developing solutions that can harness and analyze this information.

Improve Customer Relationships, Satisfaction, and Experience Through Customer Segmentation

Companies today have more information on their customers than ever before. Data are generated from not only direct interactions with the company (purchases, website visits, product registrations, call centers) but also sources such as social media, financial data, and GPS and mobile-phone use. Retailers have been able to gather increasing amounts of data to segment customers in more granular ways and then tailor advertisements and product offerings to specific customers. Companies can now identify when customers are in close proximity to the physical stores and text them special offers as an enticement. A financial institution, for example, could use data to determine which channels its customers would like to engage in and chart the optimal engagement for cross-selling and upselling. Companies can use analytics to analyze call-center information and then develop social-media campaigns that address emerging issues in short time frames.

Increase Efficiency and Profitability

Analytics teams that are led by experienced internal auditors have tremendous potential to streamline operations and reduce risk by offering business leaders greater visibility into their organizations. For companies seeking to manage global supply chains or support purchasing, analytics and data visualizations can distill huge amounts of data and analysis into easy-to-grasp dashboards and reports. In another application, large manufacturing companies use predictive analytics to manage their fleets of heavy equipment. In mining, each machine goes into the mine in order and is filled with a payload valued at around $100,000. Since there is one way in and out of the mine, if a machine breaks down it stops the line and production ceases until it can be fixed. By monitoring machines and using analytics to predict failures, the mining company can schedule preventative maintenance during off-hours, thereby increasing uptime and performance significantly.

Accelerate Speed to Market

The development of new products involves myriad variables: pharmaceuticals must manage complex clinical trials for new drugs; auto manufacturers must coordinate the design and engineering of every component in a new model; global manufacturers must deal with multiple original equipment manufacturers (OEMs) to fabricate and assemble parts for their complex machines; and consumer-electronics companies often source parts that must be manufactured to exacting specifications in China and other countries. All of these variables, as well as the human interactions throughout the process, represent data points that can provide a detailed snapshot of design and production.

A number of companies have used data and analytics to manage these complex processes and get greater insights into the choke points and patterns that can cause delays. One manufacturer used analytics techniques to highlight critical drivers of manufacturing processes. It focused on optimizing performance of the entire system, from demand planning through inventory management. By making hundreds of small improvements, the manufacturer was able to reduce costs by 50 percent, saving hundreds of millions of dollars.[3]

● ● ●

The recent evolution of data and analytics offers businesses nearly endless applications to capture more value. Such opportunities are bounded only by the imagination and a company's ability to access and analyze data. Executives seeking to unleash the power of analytics on their organizations must first ensure that they have the capabilities, processes, and talent to aggregate the data necessary to solve their business problems. The following chapter examines the digital transformation as a key enabler of analytics efforts.

Chapter

3

A DIGITAL TRANSFORMATION
TO UNLOCK ANALYTICS

*"The rapid adoption of digital technologies by
customers and competitors is disrupting every industry
and creating value at an accelerated pace."*

—Stephen Diorio, Analyst, Forbes CMO Practice

A digital transformation is one of the most powerful ways for an organization to gain a competitive advantage and position itself to pursue new opportunities. By harnessing the power of leading-edge digital technologies, business leaders can radically alter traditional business models and processes, value propositions, interactions with value-chain participants, and customer relationships.

Digital technologies also have the potential to increase the speed at which companies can respond to emerging opportunities while facilitating greater collaboration and engagement. In short, the underlying purpose of a digital transformation is to gain access to data and generate insights that will allow companies to take different kinds of actions—actions that can drastically increase efficiency, productivity, and competitiveness.

Such data-driven insights are critical for excelling in today's business environment. Failure to develop the requisite digital capabilities can result in poorly informed strategic decisions, subpar customer service, a lack of transparency into internal business processes, and fewer opportunities for improved performance. More important, since digital technologies have become table stakes, companies that drag their feet risk falling further and further behind their counterparts.

From an analytics perspective, digital technologies are foundational. Digital companies are data-driven, and their ability to access, aggregate, and analyze data provides the fuel for analytics. Of course, successful analytics efforts involve far more than technology. The right talent, culture, and business processes also are vital to enable the effective implementation and use of analytics across the organization. Traditional companies have been using analytics for decades, but a lack of access to data naturally limits the impact on the organization. One of the primary benefits of advanced analytics is that models become more precise with greater amounts of data. With less data, you can expect to produce fewer and less helpful insights.

Today, most executives are well aware of the seismic impact that digital technologies and analytics can have on their business. So the questions are: How can they make progress in integrating analytics into their operations? And how should they use these tools to generate the most value from their data?

Digital-first companies such as Amazon and Google are regularly cited as examples of how technology and data can dramatically affect business models and reshape entire industries. In practice, these points of reference provide little value for traditional companies, whose path to data and analytics often runs through legacy IT systems, disparate data sets, siloed departments, and entrenched ways of working. Thus, a digital transformation to enable analytics is an enormous undertaking. No one can do it all in one go—it's a process that must happen over time. And every organization (and industry) is at a different point in its digital maturity.

Before embarking on a digital transformation, executives must first understand where their company falls on the path to digital maturity (see exhibit 3-1). Grant Thornton has developed a five-level digital maturity framework to help executives make that determination. By assessing their organization's current capabilities, the capabilities it needs to develop, and the opportunities that greater investments in digital technologies can unlock, executives can identify the next steps they should take.

Exhibit 3-1: Companies Can Find Where They Fall on the Path to Digital Maturity

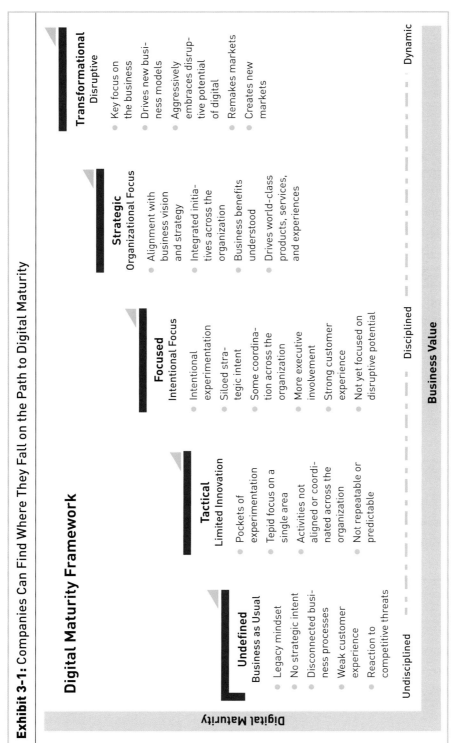

Digital Maturity Framework

Digital Maturity

Undefined
Business as Usual

- Legacy mindset
- No strategic intent
- Disconnected business processes
- Weak customer experience
- Reaction to competitive threats

Tactical
Limited Innovation

- Pockets of experimentation
- Tepid focus on a single area
- Activities not aligned or coordinated across the organization
- Not repeatable or predictable

Focused
Intentional Focus

- Intentional experimentation
- Siloed strategic intent
- Some coordination across the organization
- More executive involvement
- Strong customer experience
- Not yet focused on disruptive potential

Strategic
Organizational Focus

- Alignment with business vision and strategy
- Integrated initiatives across the organization
- Business benefits understood
- Drives world-class products, services, and experiences

Transformational
Disruptive

- Key focus on the business
- Drives new business models
- Aggressively embraces disruptive potential of digital
- Remakes markets
- Creates new markets

Undisciplined — — — Disciplined — — — Dynamic

Business Value

Source: GrantThornton

This framework can help an executive determine where to allocate resources, since moving from one phase of maturity to the next requires investments in specific capabilities. This assessment also can keep expectations realistic within the organization. While all companies might like to develop truly transformative digital capabilities, they must first lay a solid foundation upon which they can build.

Common Pitfalls on the Path to Transformation

Organizations face a daunting challenge when it comes to digital transformation. To be successful, companies must thoroughly consider a number of elements: business objectives, data from traditional and nontraditional channels, business processes, and an analytics capability to pull it all together. In addition, while analytics can help an organization quickly identify and respond to market shifts, problems, and challenges, they also require people to operate differently and with more transparency. Another key challenge, then, is getting the team on board.

Many efforts stall during the integration and timing of all of these elements. Getting the right insight to the right people at the right time is only one piece of the puzzle. Business processes and a governance model need to be in place so that the right actions can be taken within a structure that ensures consistency and quality. All of these elements need to be supported by technology.

If not done properly or executed well, a digital-transformation strategy can have a devastating impact on a business. Generating incomplete or even incorrect insights from analytics can lead to wrong and often harmful decisions. For example, an aircraft manufacturer used analytics to support its inventory and procurement. Faulty analysis indicated that certain parts would be late, leading the manufacturer to accelerate its purchases. In reality, 80 percent of the parts weren't critical to avoid disruptions, resulting in $2 billion in unnecessary spending. An organization that only partially executes will often compete against itself, and technology that does not deliver will hinder initiatives and deter success. To execute a successful digital-transformation strategy, a company must address these potential issues up front and in parallel.

A Digital-Transformation Operating Model

Digital-transformation strategies must start with a clear vision and the support of well-defined use cases. As these use cases are developed, a digital-transformation operating model can help companies build the capabilities for successful execution.

The following structured methodology is meant to walk businesses through the steps and considerations necessary to create value from a digital transformation (see exhibit 3-2). The model's six key elements ensure that business objectives, information, supporting technology, and business processes are aligned.

The operating model is a sequential process that reflects best practices in rolling out and executing a digital transformation. Organizations must have all of these elements in place—and in the proper order—to achieve business value. For internal audit departments, the forward-looking, aspirational vision must be woven into the conversation about operating models. For example, if continuous monitoring and the use of predictive modeling are central to the department's vision and success, then it must be woven into the transformation process.

Exhibit 3-2: Companies Can Follow These Steps to Ensure They Create Value from a Digital Transformation

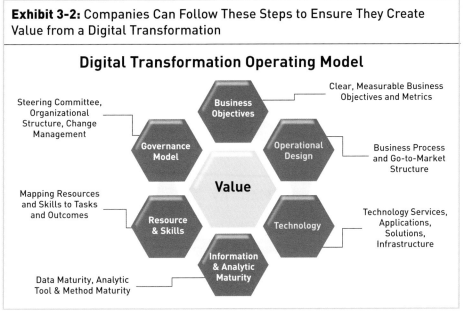

Digital Transformation Operating Model

- Steering Committee, Organizational Structure, Change Management
- Clear, Measurable Business Objectives and Metrics
- Business Process and Go-to-Market Structure
- Technology Services, Applications, Solutions, Infrastructure
- Data Maturity, Analytic Tool & Method Maturity
- Mapping Resources and Skills to Tasks and Outcomes

Governance Model · Business Objectives · Operational Design · Technology · Information & Analytic Maturity · Resource & Skills · **Value**

Source: Grant Thornton

Business Objectives

The use case's business objectives and associated value drivers are where the model starts. As part of the operating model, companies need to determine how progress will be monitored. Possibly the most important step is moving from a well-defined vision to identifying the key performance metrics that will be used to gauge progress and value. These metrics, which require access to specific information, have a direct impact on analytics models and business processes.

Operational Design

The organization needs to redesign business processes and incorporate cultural change to take action based on the insights it is seeking to generate. These elements need to work hand in hand to ensure the success of any effort; employees may need to embrace new ways of working in order to gather data and share information with the rest of the company. During a digital transformation, the organization will inevitably change and transform, so business processes need to be in place to accommodate that change.

Technology

A company's technologies need to support not only the integration of data and generation of insights but also the automation and delivery of information required for the business process. Features such as cloud-based solutions, mobile enablement, and the Internet of Things need to be seamlessly and transparently delivered to end users. At this point in the transformation model, companies should have enough clarity to invest in technologies that can support these tasks.

Information and Analytics Maturity

At this point, companies can identify the analytics insight required to produce the desired value. Companies should assess their ability to generate the analytics insight and required data. They may need to augment their internal data with external sources or partner with external parties to enhance their analytics capabilities, among other efforts.

Resources and Skills

Companies must consider what their employees need to execute all elements of the operating model. Gaps in these areas can be filled by adding or redirecting internal resources or collaborating with external organizations. Since some of the skills required are specialized—for example, experience in data science—companies may need to look to external partners and their associated resources.

Governance Model

In addition to clear executive-level buy-in and direction, a governance model provides the supporting organizational structure and management needed to address conflicts, evolve capabilities, and continually improve. Organizations often establish steering committees to help govern and facilitate these areas.

How to Get There

One of the challenges with any digital-transformation initiative is capturing the desired value. After all, such an effort can require sweeping change across every facet of the organization. Two fundamental approaches can help keep companies focused and on track: proof of value and minimum viable product. Since putting a comprehensive digital platform in place takes a great deal of time and money and can be exceedingly difficult to achieve while the company is busy operating and responding to market demands, an incremental approach is more realistic for most companies. By selecting a series of use cases, companies can effectively build a road map to a comprehensive transformation. Each completed use case becomes another piece of the foundation to a transformation.

Through these use cases, companies can steadily generate value from their investments in digital technologies. The key is to select viable use cases. Once a use case is defined, organizations can determine its viability and the potential for capturing the desired value by following a two-step process.

Proof of value: This tactic uses quick sprints (six- to eight-week efforts) to evaluate a use case. For example, suppose a company is seeking to identify customers who are most likely to purchase additional products or services. To do so, it can develop a scoring system that prioritizes customers on the basis of financial, loyalty, and market data. Proof of value would involve quickly integrating a representative set of historical data, building the analytical models, and producing results that can be judged against what actually happened.

Minimum viable product (MVP): Once a use case is proved, the fastest and best way to begin capturing value is by developing an MVP. As the name suggests, it is the most basic solution and target operating model that can provide the defined capability and allow the organization to begin to capture value. The organization can add enhancements and additional functionality over time; companies typically introduce new features in 90- to 180-day cycles. In the above example, an MVP may provide the sales organization a score prioritizing clients that have a greater propensity to purchase additional products or services based on a few data sources. Over time, that solution may incorporate more data from the customer, social media, and market data to enhance the models, provide heat maps on each client, and even proactively identify and market to customers based on specific offerings.

The use case, the solution, and the target operating model mature throughout the process (see exhibit 3-3).

In the example on page 33, the organization focuses on each area of the operating model in sequence along the road map. At any given step in the process, the organization addresses and refines elements of the use case, strategy, solution, and target operating model. The quantity of use cases that an organization can have in flight at any given time is dependent on its capabilities across the target operating model.

For many organizations, expanding capacity through the effective use of partnerships is critical. For example, technology partnerships could enable the organization to deliver a cloud-based capability quickly as an operational expense. Partnerships in the analytical space also are important. By tapping the expertise of companies with deep analytics capabilities, an organization can quickly enhance its analytics maturity while taking advantage of the partners' deep subject-matter expertise.

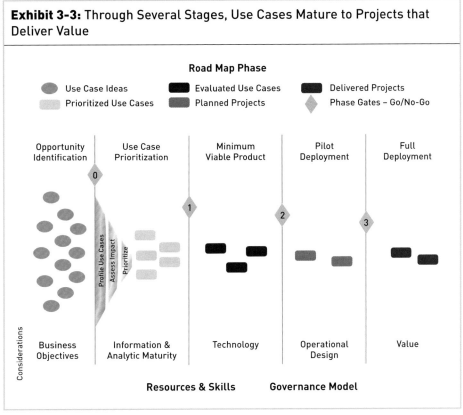

Exhibit 3-3: Through Several Stages, Use Cases Mature to Projects that Deliver Value

Source: GrantThornton

For their part, internal audit members must work toward their digital and analytics goals every day—both to make it a part of their core function and to ensure that progress continues (see sidebar, "Promoting the Use of New Analytics in Internal Audit"). This team also should reassess and reprioritize its use of analytics at least every quarter. A willingness to evolve can help the organization stay relevant as circumstances and goals change.

Promoting the Use of New Analytics in Internal Audit

In a recent study we conducted, a mere 13 percent of internal audit professionals reported strong analytics competencies within their internal audit teams. How should teams combat this deficiency? Many organizations have employed innovative programs to encourage and expand the use of analytics in internal audit. One company interviewed, for instance, runs a company-wide guest program that invites experts in specific areas, such as artificial intelligence (AI), to join other project teams to help them explore the use of new analytics. For example, AI coders have teamed up with internal audit to increase efficiency and develop new audit methods.[1]

Sprint has explored similar programs. It creates technology audit group (TAG) teams that are intended to increase collaboration and innovation within the company's internal audit department. TAG teams support areas with the potential to drive value across internal audit and with auditors. The company has developed TAG teams that focus on data analytics, internal audit process improvement, auditor development, and fraud. Internal audit employees can join TAG teams based on their interest and expertise. For teams requiring oversight from SMEs—for example, data analytics and fraud teams—an internal audit SME, such as a data scientist or certified fraud examiner, provides oversight to the TAG team members. Then the TAG team members are embedded into individual audit-testing teams to ensure consistency, quality, and value.[2]

Critical Success Factors

As companies get started, a few factors will determine or hinder success. To execute a successful digital transformation, an organization must embrace the following ideals and mind-sets.

Executive Leadership

Top leadership needs to understand and communicate the vision for the digital transformation and the value of analytics to the organization.

Business-Process Alignment

Leaders must align frontline efforts and the boardroom on culture and the business processes that support the transformation.

A Fail-Fast Model

Companies should develop new ideas quickly and change course as they succeed or fail. One way to determine whether an analytics project will move forward or conclude is to test the preliminary outcomes and analytics with end users and key stakeholders to determine the degree to which the solution meets their needs. Leaders shouldn't be afraid to fail; if an effort fails, fail fast and recover quickly.

Customer-Centric Strategy

Maintain interaction with customers to remain close to their needs and interests. All business-model and process changes must be geared toward improving the customer experience.

A Digital Culture

Understand the impact of digital technology, and spread that knowledge throughout the organization.

With these critical success factors in mind, and an understanding of the digital transformation operating model, companies will be well on their way to changing the way they do business and conceptualizing success and growth. Rather than being deterred by the enormity of the digital transformation, executives should instead focus on individual use cases that can enable them to build the necessary capabilities gradually. And they should focus on making improvements incrementally based on feedback, every single day.

Given the importance of use cases in propelling the digital transformation and generating value, selecting the best use cases will be critical. The next chapter offers a proven framework to vet and prioritize potential efforts so that companies can focus only on those opportunities with the most promise—and the biggest potential to create value.

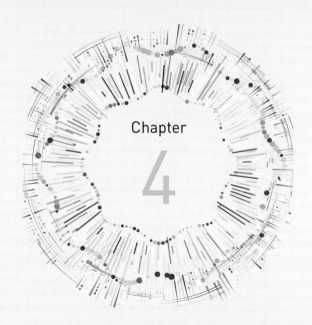

Chapter

4

HOW TO REALIZE VALUE FROM AN ANALYTICS PROGRAM: DEFINING, SCORING, AND DETERMINING PRIORITIES

"It is not a daily increase but a daily decrease.
Hack away at the inessentials."

—BRUCE LEE

The demand for analytics capacity within an organization will likely outstrip its capacity (or supply). Thus, selecting the most promising projects is critical.

Companies that start an analytics project from a data or statistical perspective often struggle to embed insights into the normal business process. Starting a project with business objectives in mind is a much more effective approach. And those objectives should align with the company's overarching strategy. Defining, scoring, and determining objectives should bring the company's priorities into focus.

First Steps to Creating Value

To achieve the most possible value from analytics projects, companies must start with the following four tasks.

Define the Business Problem

Without a specific business problem to solve, an analytics project is likely to fail. Many projects start with a focus on data or at the direction of a sponsor or leader. Data are integrated, analytics applied, and results provided. These might be good "analytical" results, but they have little to do with solving a real business problem. Without clear objectives and metrics, insights are likely to be incomplete, incorrect, or not actionable. For example, we interviewed a data scientist who was working on a large analytics project for his company. While the insights he was generating seemed phenomenal from his perspective, they didn't match the business's strategic priorities. Clearer direction at the project's inception could have produced a better result. Likewise, analytics teams must include individual contributors who have connections at the leadership level to confirm the direction of the project. These connections can create more transparency into the organization's broader goals and ensure that the team doesn't waste time on an effort that does not contribute value (see sidebar "Collaborating on Analytics to Add Value at Fifth Third Bank").

Collaborating on Analytics to Add Value at Fifth Third Bank

At Fifth Third Bank, senior and predictive business managers lead a team of four analytics experts to apply data analytics across the audit function, increase the scope of audit, and use data analytics to test whole operations. In this focused effort, the team works directly with internal audit data analytics champions who understand data, processes, and systems to create a shared approach to analytics. The team also provides training to internal audit on how to pull data sets and use company tools to analyze them, ensuring all have the required skills and are focused on efforts that add value.

Define the Insights Needed

Once the business metrics are clearly defined, the company must define the insights it needs to deliver value. This is another area where projects often derail. Actionable insight is defined in business terms; it is not the output of an analytical model. For example, a production supervisor responsible for keeping a plant up and running might need insights such as:

- Which pieces of equipment are at risk of failure within a given time period? That is, can I wait for the scheduled maintenance, or do I need to address this at shift change?

- Which at-risk pieces of equipment are critical to production? How can I prioritize my actions?

- How do I optimize the downtime? Can I address multiple problems in the same period?

To address some of these questions and determine the necessary insights, companies can consider the business imperatives and analytics that would enable changes to be made in different categories (see exhibit 4-1).

Knowing which insights are necessary will help the data scientist determine the best analytics methods to produce them. Absent a holistic view of the business problem and the data available for analytics, it is difficult (or impossible) for a company to devise a clear strategy to produce meaningful, integrated, and actionable insights.

Narrow the Data

Successful analytics projects depend on a clear understanding of the data required to achieve the desired insights. One common mistake is to pull together all of the different data sets for analysis without narrowing them down beforehand. This error leads to extra effort and long delays in the deployment of analytics. It also reduces the team's odds of success because members are wasting time on information that may be unnecessary or irrelevant.

Exhibit 4-1: Business Imperatives, Analytics Enablement, and Enterprise Components Vary Across the Industrial Value Chain

Analytics in the Industrial Value Chain

	Intelligent Design Engineering & Quality	Intelligent Supply Chain	Intelligent Manufacturing	Intelligent Workplace	Intelligent Aftermarket	Intelligent Services
Business Imperatives	• Lifecycle Management • Faster Time to Market • Improved Quality	• Fewer Interruptions • Reduced Cost • Reduce Risk	• Improved Quality • Better Efficiency • Higher Throughout • Reduce Energy Waste	• Intelligent & Secure Facilities • Green Buildings • Worker Productivity & Safety	• Lifecycle Management • Disintermediation • Customer Intimacy • Brand Loyalty	• New Digital Offerings • Intelligent Revenue Models
Analytic Enablement	• Rapid Prototyping • Experimental Design Focus • Product Usage Insights • Asset/Product Performance Data	• Transparent & Flexible Supply Chain • Inventory Management • Supplier Quality & Risk Management	• Asset Monitoring & Predictive Maintenance • Product Quality Tracking • Smart Energy Usage	• Space & Energy Utilization & Planning Analytics • Worker Productivity & Safety Tracking • Instant Delivery of Information & Resources to Workers	• Product & Usage Insights • Aftermarket Services • Predict	• Differentiated Product Services/Features • Customer Tailored Product Upgrades • Usage-Based Revenue Models

Enterprise Components: Mobile · Wearables · Weather · Social · Experiential Design · Instrumentation & Connectivity · Standards · Enterprise Platform · Cloud · Data Strategy · Big Data · Analytics · Securit · Compliance

Source: Grant Thornton

40

Achieve Operational Readiness

Maintaining objectivity about the organization's ability to take action is another area where companies struggle. To be operationally ready, a company must have business processes in place, an understanding of the impact of employing analytics across the enterprise, a clear definition of the resources required, and a plan for dealing with unexpected consequences. For example, if the analytics predict that a piece of your equipment could fail, do you have a business process to address that predictive insight? The process may include alerting the client, incurring additional costs to fix a problem that has not occurred yet, and understanding the potential liability of failing to act.

How to Define, Score, and Prioritize Analytics Projects

A phased approach to defining and prioritizing analytics projects can improve the chances they will succeed and allow companies to produce insights that have business value. The proven development approach discussed here allows companies to be agile and quickly identify and generate value through an iterative, continuous-improvement process with four steps: develop the vision, define the use case, score the use case, and scope the use case (see exhibit 4-2). When considering analytics priorities, a company starts with innumerable, sometimes overwhelming, options. Following these steps will help a company prioritize those options, determine the most viable, identify potential flaws, and build internal support in the process.

Exhibit 4-2: Four Steps Are the Key to Prioritizing Analytics Projects

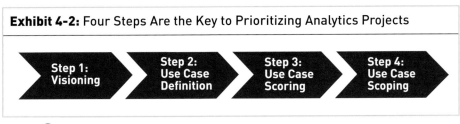

Source: Grant Thornton

Step 1: Develop a Vision for the Use Case

When evaluating potential analytics projects, the organization needs to have a common understanding of how such projects can produce value for the company. Vision-development sessions help teams determine how analytics will help produce incremental revenue, transform the business model, and innovate. These brainstorm-like sessions focus on a conversation about the potential value of various opportunities. Typically, companies use design thinking or rapid use case development (or both) to help them develop their vision.

- **Design thinking**—This methodology draws on logic, imagination, and intuition to explore possibilities and benefits for the company, business unit, and end user or customer.

- **Rapid use case development**—Rapid workshops help companies quickly explore potential use cases to solve their critical business problems.

Using these techniques to develop a vision results in the identification of potential use cases. Informing this discussion of use cases is a set of criteria to help the team come to a consensus and common understanding of how to assess opportunities (see exhibit 4-3). Together they can then identify and prioritize analytics projects that will have maximum business impact. Once the potential use cases have been evaluated according to the vision-development criteria, an enterprise-level analytics agenda can be created to map leadership priorities and create an executable and agreed-upon road map.

Exhibit 4-3: Select Criteria Can Aid in Teams' Assessment of Their Vision

Analytics in the Industrial Value Chain

Individual Selection Criteria

Business Impact
- Acquire new customers
- Drive brand loyalty
- Increase share of wallet
- Drive customer satisfaction

Risk
- Process: ability to leverage
- People: ability to adopt
- Technology: ease of execution

Cost & Complexity
- IT implementation costs
- Deployment costs
- Infrastructure investment

IT & Data
- Available software assets
- Data availability
- Data quality
- Data interconnectedness
- Required skillset

Organization Readiness
- Ability to successfully embed in current processes
- Degree of resistance to change

Dependency & Synergy Criteria

Synergies
- Data requirements
- Tooling
- IT structure
- Business structures
- Common solutions – one to many

Dependencies
- Data dependencies
- Infrastructure dependencies
- Process dependencies
- Organizational readiness
- Competing initiatives
- Sequencing initiatives based on building blocks/ capability evolution

Strategic Fit Selection Criteria

Strategic Fit
- Leadership vision
- Industry imperatives
- "Must win battles"
- Transformation strategy – i.e., "sharp pencil decision-making"

Source: Grant Thornton

Step 2: Define the Use Case

Each use case is intended to frame and solve a specific business problem and identify the business value that it will produce. After loosely identifying a handful of opportunities in the vision-development workshop (a more qualitative exercise), teams can hold use case workshops to help them summarize and define preliminary use cases and the business objectives for each. This process should help the team narrow the opportunities to four use cases—a manageable and realistic starting point. For each use case, the process includes the following components (see exhibit 4-4):

- **Hypothesis**: A clear statement about the vision for a use case and its objectives

- **Stakeholders**: Executives, sponsors, and business leaders who will benefit from the insights and dedicate resources to define the required insights

- **Value drivers**: Elements that will result in the creation of value

  - Level 1 – Definition of the overall value that will be created

  - Level 2 – Definition of the value that will be derived by stakeholders seeking specific actionable insights

- **Analytics insights**: Insights, in business terms, that are needed to address the previously defined value drivers

- **Data inputs**: The data that will be used to generate the required insights (known as "data in context")

- **Success criteria**: How the use case will be judged—that is, what will success look like?

- **Roles and responsibilities**: The obligations of employees who participate in the process to determine and prioritize the use cases

Exhibit 4-4: Teams Collect Key Information, Such as Value Drivers and Insights, for Each Use Case

Hypothesis & Scenario: Leverage machine data to improve operator productivity and conformance

Stakeholders: Elevators, escalators, motors, pumps, aircraft & engines, buildings & internal systems, commercial equipment

Value Drivers – Level 1	Value Drivers – Level 2	Analytics Insights	Data Inputs
Enhance value proposition Minimize machine abuse New services revenue stream	Higher operator productivity and competency Better equipment utilization Better manpower planning (leveraging better understanding of workforce and their competitors) Safer operations Enabler to operator incentive model Improved predictability of site productivity Decrease training cost Decrease maintenance cost	Assess operator productivity based on conditions Understand and benchmark operators to guide training recommendations and coaching Provide operator with feedback to improve performance Site-to-site application profile Operator scorecard (including safety) Shift management guidance	Machine data Operations data Training logs Dealer service calls Work order history

Key Elements	Description
Success Criteria:	
Roles & Responsibilities:	

Source: Grant Thornton

Step 3: Score the Use Case

Once a use case is defined, the team should conduct an objective scoring exercise to help define staffing and resource requirements and enable the team to compare use cases by the amount of resources needed to generate insights (see exhibit 4-5). This process can be broken down into three broad elements: business value, operational readiness, and strategic importance. Each of the use cases should be assigned a value of 0 (least) to 5 (most) for each of the following elements and measures:

Business Value

- **Quantifiable and measurable**: Is the business value of the use case quantifiable and measurable?

- **Size of value**: What is the quantifiable business value expected by stakeholders?

- **Net revenue stream**: Will the use case drive revenue?

Operational Readiness

- **Use case definition**: Is the use case—including the business value drivers—clearly defined?

- **Business process alignment**: Are the business process and operations of the use case aligned with the strategies and activities of the business?

- **Informational readiness**: Do we have the data and information we need to proceed with the use case?

Strategic Importance

- **Competitive advantage**: Will the use case create a competitive advantage?

- **Market transformation**: Will the use case be perceived as transformational in the market?

- **Executive sponsorship**: Does the use case have verified executive sponsorship?

Exhibit 4-5: Scoring Enables a Team to Understand the Resources Necessary for Each Use Case

Priority Metric	Measure	Value (0-5)
Business Value	Quantifiable	4
	Measurable	5
	Net Revenue Stream	4
	Subtotal	13
Operational Readiness	Use Case Defined	5
	Business Process Alignment (Process + Confidence)	3
	Informational Readiness	3
	Subtotal	11
Strategic Importance	Competitive Advantage	3
	Market Transformation	4
	Executive Sponsorship	3
	Subtotal	11
	Total	35

Source: Grant Thornton

Use cases should then be ranked by score and prioritized based on the business problems and opportunities that they address.

Step 4: Scope the Use Case

Scoping is the last step in the process. It helps teams understand all that's needed to execute the analytics project. Teams must verify the availability of data and ensure that the scope of the use case can be clearly defined. Elements that need to be defined during scoping include:

- **User experience**: Review all analytics insights to be derived from the use case and outline deliverables and the user experience expected for each.

- **Data integration**: Evaluate all data sources, elements, source systems, quality of data, and approximate size of all data sets.

- **Roles and responsibilities**: Assign individuals to lead the following work streams: project management, data entry, analytics build, solution design, functional testing, user screens, and dashboards.

- **Project timeline**: Lay out a detailed project timeline that includes key milestones.

- **Project deliverables**: Outline specific project deliverables aligned to the timeline.

● ● ●

The selection of the best use cases—those that provide tangible business value—is critical to the success of analytics projects. Once the team has defined, scored, and scoped its use cases, it should execute them in order of priority using a phased approach. A "proof of value" should be performed within a defined timeline (for example, 30 to 60 days) to determine if the data can be used to generate the insights being sought. Internal audit can add the most value by assessing the process for selecting use cases, including control risks, audit control, and project-specific risks and use analytics to mitigate them.

As discussed, prioritizing use cases depends in part on the availability of data. Companies must understand not only where their data reside and how to aggregate them but also how to combine different data sets in order to uncover patterns and insights that might otherwise be hidden. The next chapter details various ways to create blended data sets.

Chapter

5

DETECTING TRENDS AND PATTERNS THROUGH BLENDED DATA

*"If you just focus on the smallest details, you
never get the big picture right."*

—Leroy Hood

Most organizational leaders understand how to analyze individual data sources to extract insights. For example, U.S. military recruiters are able to narrow down 320 million Americans to just those who are most likely to join the military by using a single piece of information—men aged 18 to 21. With this one source of data, recruiters narrowed their focus by almost 98 percent, to just eight million Americans.

But what if military recruiters could narrow their focus even more? By understanding the predictive ability of multiple, specific data sources, analysts can blend those sources and multiply the utility of their analysis.

It's possible for a company to take the data it has—including some sources it doesn't even realize it has—and maximize their accuracy and therefore their value. These military recruiters, for instance, already knew that getting potential recruits to attend in-person meetings is the single best way to guarantee success. What if they could predict which of these eight million Americans would be open to such face-to-face meetings? And what if they knew how to appeal specifically to them? To do so, they needed more information and more context. They needed to combine data sources to figure out these individuals' motivations and target others who might have similar motivations.

The recruiters held focus groups with 60 18- to 21-year-olds to gather more data and analyze their motivation. Why were they joining? The focus groups revealed that some recruits were interested in the challenge, some were drawn to the stability, and still others planned to use veterans' benefits to continue their education. Each indicator on its own is predictive, but used together, the value is much greater. With this information, the recruiters could get in front of potential recruits, frame their marketing material more deliberately, and develop a pitch that would better connect with potential recruits (see exhibit 5-1).

Therein lies the potential of blending data. Combining data sets reveals innovative ways to tackle challenges, whether that means boosting efficiency or better predicting future behavior.

How Blended Data Better Predict Behavior

For more than a decade, analysts have used the term "data integration" to describe the methods they used to combine data from multiple sources and make them accessible across the business units of a large enterprise through a data warehouse. Data blending, however, is much more. It involves identifying multiple data sources and using them together to develop innovative ways to approach old problems—and it can be a game changer.

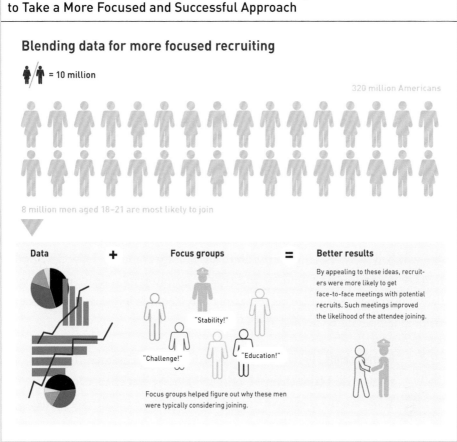

Exhibit 5-1: By Combining Sources of Data, Military Recruiters Were Able to Take a More Focused and Successful Approach

Blending data for more focused recruiting

= 10 million

320 million Americans

8 million men aged 18–21 are most likely to join

Data + **Focus groups** = **Better results**

By appealing to these ideas, recruiters were more likely to get face-to-face meetings with potential recruits. Such meetings improved the likelihood of the attendee joining.

"Stability!"

"Challenge!" "Education!"

Focus groups helped figure out why these men were typically considering joining.

Source: ◉ GrantThornton

This may seem relatively simple on its face: put the right data sources together and they can create much more accurate predictions. One key challenge for most organizations, however, is determining which data sets are the *right* ones. Sometimes the connections are obvious. For instance, if an auto insurance company combines three sources of data—demographics (age/gender), past incident history (accidents/other claims), and vehicle value (to estimate the cost of repairs)—the enhanced accuracy compared with taking each of these variables independently allows the company to pinpoint estimates for policies to maximize profits.

In other scenarios, however, it's far more challenging to identify which of the common dimensions across disparate data sources will help answer a specific question. A large brokerage firm, for example, jumped into data analysis thinking it had selected sources that would get results. The firm is now beginning its third iteration of this process, having turned up interesting findings in previous efforts but still lacking actionable recommendations from the analysis.

With data blending, each stream of data answers a question. If enough questions are answered, the team can make more accurate predictions and act accordingly.

A big-box retailer, for example, was struggling to improve its supply chain performance. The availability of the right products when a customer is in the store ultimately makes or breaks a sale. But carrying too much inventory wastes space and ties up cash—which in some cases sounds the death knell for the company. How can a retailer determine the appropriate amount and type of inventory? An analyst working on behalf of the retailer identified six indicators that would help the company identify what products would be needed and when:

1. **Overall trends**: How long has the store been operational? Is it in a stable area? Has it changed its hours? Does it ever change its hours? What are the traffic patterns in the area? Have the demographics in the area changed?

2. **Purchase trends**: How much of this product has it sold in the past? Are sales increasing or decreasing?

3. **Weather**: Does weather affect the sale of this product? What weather is expected?

4. **Social media**: Is there a social-media buzz surrounding this product or product group?

5. **Promotions**: Are there currently sales or other marketing promotions for this product?

6. **Competition**: Has competition recently changed for this product? Are competitors opening stores nearby? Are competitors currently running sales or other marketing promotions for this product? Are they running a promotion for a similar or competing product at nearby locations?

Each of these indicators on its own was predictive, but used together, their value was much greater. By blending the data gathered from these indicators, the analyst was able to more accurately predict the next period's sales. Thus, the retailer was able to reduce the number of product outages by 8 percent and decrease excess inventory—the number of unneeded products on its shelves—by almost 5 percent. For a national chain managing tens of thousands of stores, these savings were considerable.

Get More Value Out of the Data Sets You Already Have

Indeed, blended data can do much more than improve supply chain performance. It also can empower financial decision making and improve overall business performance. In finance, for example, common data sources from financial systems—such as general ledgers, AP files, and payment files, among others—are often used as a single source for analyzing situations. Despite the depth of detail in these data sources, this tried-and-true method of determining high-risk financial transactions has the same limitations as other analytics projects that rely on just one data source. Without the additional layers and perspectives that other internal and external data sets can bring, companies won't be able to fully connect the dots (see sidebar, "Expanding the Function of Core Data at a Fortune 500 Company").

Times change and industries adapt. The data sources common to all organizations, including the general ledger, can now be used to support descriptive analytics of processes while setting the stage for predictive analysis.

> ## Expanding the Function of Core Data at a Fortune 500 Company
>
> A Fortune 500 company that was interviewed cited continuous expansion of its capabilities and exploration of new ways to use its data in order to address constantly changing needs. The company believes the value of analytics will increase as analytics capabilities evolve. In addition, it recognizes that analytics tools may change but the data warehouse will not. While the IT team owns the data warehouse, they share it with other teams to allow the company's core data to be used in a flexible way. If finance or internal audit has a need for certain data, they request access, and this request is reviewed by a small cross-functional team. Once approved, the team is granted custom views of the data.

Extracting Deeper Perspectives from General Ledgers

General ledgers are the lifeblood of an organization, supporting its financial reporting. The ledger also provides insights into the nature of financial processes, from the perspective of timing, quality, and efficiency.

A general ledger is much like a checkbook register but far more detailed. In most accounting systems, each journal entry in the ledger is a robust financial document retaining many of the details of the original transaction. Therefore, a revenue-related journal entry may show not only the amount of the transaction but also the customer number, operational statistics, and location where the transaction took place. Internal auditors, sales directors, operations officers, inventory-management personnel, and others can transform general ledgers into useful trend analyses through several approaches.

Searching for Unusual Changes in Trial and Ledger Balances

Most financial-reporting managers and auditors perform vertical and horizontal analyses of trial balances for each account number. They generally do these analyses annually, but they could easily scan for trends monthly. A more granular perspective—a month or a week versus a year—allows for an analysis of more balances per general ledger account and may reveal unusual changes that would be masked at an annual or quarterly level.

A weekly breakdown, for instance, might uncover exceptionally good or bad days in certain accounts (see exhibit 5-2). With this closer look, auditors can isolate specific locations, people, and time frames that may require or benefit from additional focus.

Exhibit 5-2: Breaking Data Down into Shorter Time Frames Paints a More Accurate Picture of Trends and Activity

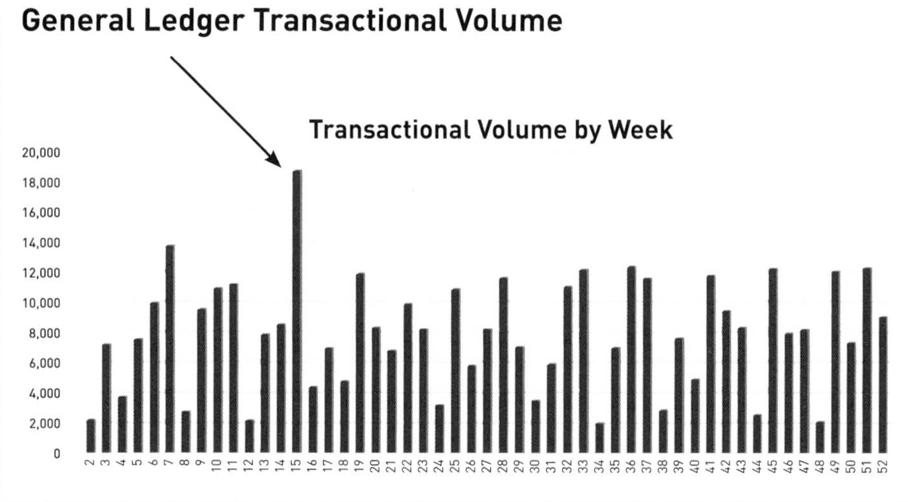

General Ledger Transactional Volume

Transactional Volume by Week

Source: ◉ GrantThornton

What's more, instead of simply analyzing balances, auditors may summarize monthly general ledger postings by account. For most, this approach would yield surprising results and help financial reporting managers to better understand their activity and see it from a different perspective.

Understanding Who is Posting and at What Volume

In the spirit of attaining a new perspective, summarizing ledger details by user—in other words, by who enters or approves each entry—essentially provides a process map of journal entries by user. Knowing the number of entries posted and approved by user can be extremely useful from a controls perspective, particularly as it also can show trends. If one user enters inventory-cost entries all day long and then suddenly posts a fixed-asset addition, that disparity could indicate an error or perhaps even nefarious activity. Financial-reporting directors also can use this information to understand the level of work being performed at a given location compared with others and adjust personnel management accordingly.

Finding Trends in Revenues and Expenses by Location

Subledger sales-management systems often post daily revenues and expenditures by location. While analytics teams may be inclined to dive right into the subledger systems for analysis, the general ledger data can be a good starting point as well, acting as a benchmark for the subledger data trends. In essence, the daily sales postings to the subledgers should agree with the general ledger. If they don't, it may indicate that all sales are not being recorded in a complete and timely fashion, which could result in inaccuracies.

In addition, trends in general-ledger revenues and expenses can be statistically analyzed by month in relation to the prior year. Year-on-year trends in the average and standard deviation of sales by month and location, for example, can help identify locations with increased or decreased volatility in sales transactions. This knowledge can help audit teams identify fraudulent revenue postings while identifying unusual patterns for sales directors to consider in their site visits.

Aligning Other Independent Variables

Beyond summarizing sales by month, additional independent operational variables may be applied to assess the changes over time and whether they are reasonable. For example, in an oil and gas analysis, heating degree days, as tracked by the National Oceanic and Atmospheric Administration, could be added to a regression model to assess the correlation of heating degree days to the increases or decreases in revenue over time. Heating degree days is a measure of the degrees it takes to heat a home to an average temperature, which was used to assess residential consumption of gas. Using this approach, it was possible to obtain a significant correlation. To build a stronger regression model on multiple factors, analysts also could include other independent variables such as customers by location, gallons sold by location, and population density near the location.

Learn to Work with Unstructured Data

While structured data are captured neatly in columns and rows, unstructured data have no predefined manner or format (see sidebar, "The Difference Between Structured and Unstructured Data"). According to the global market-intelligence firm International Data Corporation, unstructured data account for nearly 90 percent of all enterprise data. To be successful in the future, analytics must take different types of data into account.

The Difference Between Structured and Unstructured Data

Structured data exist in an understandable, organized format that allows the data to be fed into a relational database-management system for analysis. Operational data from an enterprise resource planning application, transactional data, customer data, financial data, and other data that include specific information (such as names, dates, addresses, and payment amounts) are all examples of structured data.

Unstructured data have no predefined organizing format. They are typically displayed in a free-form, text-heavy format that makes any type of in-depth analysis much more difficult. Examples of unstructured data include call-center communications, open-text fields, contracts, audio and video, machine-generated data (server logs), blogs, and most social-media feeds (such as Facebook, LinkedIn, or Twitter). Email, for example, is indexed by date, time, sender, recipient, and subject, but the body of an email is an unstructured open-text field.

To derive useful insights from unstructured data, analysts must first prepare and transform the data so they can be structured and analyzed. According to CIO Insight, the steps in analyzing unstructured data include the following:[1]

> 1) Choose only the most relevant sources, keeping in mind the goals and desired end result. An organization's existing technology must be able to support both the project's information architecture and the ability to process a real-time stream of data.
>
> 2) Next, the data must be prepared for storage by removing noise such as blank spaces and symbols and then changing strings of text into formal language.
>
> 3) Once the language is standardized, it is possible to establish relationships among sources and design a structured database where an analyst may use the frequency of named entities such as people, companies, and geographies to understand patterns. Then the data may be classified, segmented, and fed into data analytics tools.

In other words, given that a majority of data are text, data analysts must break free from their habitual desire to look only at the 0s and 1s. Take, for example, a general ledger filled with journal entries that can be organized into two types:

1. *Number fields*: Journal number, account number, debit or credit amount, enterer ID number, and journal date. These fields may represent 50 characters in any given transaction record.

2. *Text fields*: Journal description, account name, enterer name, and line description. Given their text-based nature, these fields would represent 250 characters in any given transaction record.

While numbers are generally a factor in the date and value of transactions, textual notes fill in all of the open spaces from many perspectives—telling us about the who, what, where, and why. In the above example, assuming a total record length of 300 characters, the number fields would represent less than 20 percent of the total data in the file, but, paradoxically, they are typically the main focus of a financial professional's summarizations, duplicate analysis, and other statistical analysis. By expanding their analysis beyond numbers to text, financial professionals will find not just more data but also higher-quality data.

Textual analytics is a new field for many organizations, and internal audit teams are poised to capitalize on this area given their unique position in their companies. These teams have access to all available data sets within the company and can act as a clearinghouse for some of the key words to search within these data sets. Text analytics is working largely with unstructured data, using an approach where the key terms are identified by summarizing all of the words. For example, in a search of data sets for "corruption," internal auditors might use key terms such as "facilitation payment." But in summarizing the unstructured data, they may find that "FP" or "facpay" also are associated with corrupt payments. Internal auditors can maximize this expanding technique by accessing a variety of data sources, such as:

- Social media
- Contracts (for example, leases, sales, and vendors)
- Purchase and sales orders
- Process memos
- Email communication

Text-analytics solutions can summarize words used in the general ledger journal descriptions to assess, for instance, year-over-year word changes that may signal changes in operational or financial processes. They also can identify repeated uses of key phrases that may raise concerns from a financial-reporting standpoint (such as "adjust" or "reclass") or from a corruption standpoint (such as "facilitation payment" or "sales consultation"). Text-analytics solutions also can review text from public sources to summarize both the words and the positive or negative sentiments of important documents such as earnings releases and financial filings. Analysts also may compare their own companies' public documents with those of their peers.

How to Blend and Enrich Data

Armed with a greater awareness of the sources and types of data, companies can focus on combining data sets to enhance visibility into specific parts of the organization. To start, companies should ensure they have the technology and processes to capture data from all areas of the enterprise. Once a specific use case is defined, companies can determine which data sets are needed to generate the required insights. For example, a bank that is seeking to promote its home-mortgage products to its existing customer base might pull data that segment accounts by balance and by the account holder's age. It also might add data on customer engagement by channel (in person, online, mobile banking) to determine the best way to reach out. And the bank also could examine geographic data and real estate information by zip code to understand the level of activity in the market.

The bank would capture and store these data and build a database infrastructure to house new data. Once the data are integrated, the bank could analyze different data sources to detect trends and patterns—for example, the age at which customers first apply for mortgages and average income at application. The bank could use that data to develop a profile of the target customer and predict when customers would be ready to consider purchasing a home. The bank's data scientists would then determine correlation or causation in the analysis. From these results, the bank could implement a program to reach out to targeted customers—say, individuals aged 27 to 32 within an income range in a certain zip code—with offers through its mobile banking app. As part of this effort, the bank would have to consider privacy issues, particularly regarding data from unstructured social media.

In general, the different combinations of data and potential analytics are limited only by the number of data sources and the ability and imagination of data scientists. A company's approach to blended data should be closely aligned with use-case and business objectives.

● ● ●

Using singular data sources—a common practice across industries—provides companies with partial answers. It's important to look back and understand what has happened, which is easy enough with singular data sources. But without knowing *why* these things have happened, companies cannot take action, progress, or keep pace with competitors.

Once a company has determined which data to use and how to bring different sources together to get even more insights, the next step is to ensure it's getting the insights it set out to find. How does a company measure its efforts to make sure it's accomplishing its goals? The next chapter details how to assess efforts in terms of time, cost, and quality.

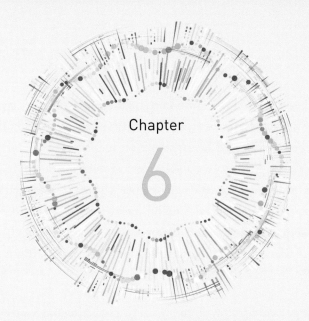

Chapter

6

HOW TO MEASURE THE
VALUE OF ANALYTICS

*"If you've come this far, maybe you're
willing to come a little further."*

—From *The Shawshank Redemption*

So reads a note in the countryside left for Red by Andy DuFresne toward the end of the movie, *The Shawshank Redemption*. This sentiment has particular resonance for organizations that have sought to integrate analytics into their organization. Too many companies declare victory when they have finished building their analytics capabilities. In fact, in a recent survey of internal audit professionals we conducted, 80 percent of respondents stated that they do not measure the value generated from investments in analytics. But building capability is just the start of an ongoing effort to ensure that investments in analytics are paying off. Once people in an organization learn of a new analytics capability, demand for it is likely to far outstrip supply. Just as company leaders need to evaluate and prioritize use cases on the front end (see chapter 4), the organization needs to measure the impact and value achieved on the back end.

As companies pursue an unbiased assessment of their analytics, they typically employ multiple maturity models to rate their efforts on a variety of numeric scales. A useful assessment measures how well the organization uses analytics to increase revenue, reduce costs, optimize performance, and improve decision making. While the resulting scores could provide bragging rights among peers, such an approach also can leave an organization still searching for a useful measurement of the ROI. Companies sometimes resist undertaking more multidimensional measurement because they are reluctant to face what the audit might reveal. Still, calculating ROI is an important component of a sustainable analytics program.

In this chapter, we take a pragmatic approach to addressing the concerns of financial professionals about justifying their companies' investments in analytics. To that end, measuring analytics follows the pattern for any project for which concerns include quality, time, and cost (in other words, any project). In assessing the value of an organization's analytics projects, these factors are referred to as:

1. Quality of decision making
2. Speed to insights
3. Return on investment

Of course, a project's overall objectives—such as greater efficiency, cost savings, and performance—will determine the relative importance of each of these metrics. Companies must clearly define what they hope to achieve and then select the right indicators to gauge progress and success.

The Quality of Decision Making

While speed may be the most exciting aspect of analytics to track, there is no benefit to an organization if a speedy result leads to a poor decision. Quality is paramount and must be considered at every step of the analytics measurement process, from data acquisition to the resulting insights. If the measurement process is to result in a useful analytic, quality must be a function of each component.

Data Acquisition

The analytics team needs to understand the table structure of data acquired from any given system. Understanding the base data is the first step in assessing how to use the data to formulate a hypothesis and establish a foundation for subsequent work. Further, the methods by which the data are entered into that structure, such as through an accounting system, need to be understood in detail, because different organizations, and groups within them, have their own customs and practices.

For example, a company may use a common enterprise software system to manage sales, but the types of document codes used and how they are entered determine how the data should be acquired before they are entered by the analytics engine. One company may use a document code associated with freight on a sale, while another has no freight and uses the same document code for commission payments. If the team does not understand such foundational aspects of the data, the analysis could be highly inaccurate.

Data Completeness and Entry

If data extractions from a system are incomplete or inaccurate, the scope of the data's analysis will be limited. If data are not complete, the team might try to extrapolate its analysis results to apply to a larger potential population—and such approaches, unless a statistical sampling model is employed, are questionable at best. Complete data sets establish a scope from which hypotheses can be tested.

Some common techniques for testing the completeness of a data set include:

1. Summarizing transactions by month to ensure that each month is represented in the data

2. Comparing record and batch value totals of data extracts with those in the system data tables

3. Testing physical documents, such as invoices received from external parties, against internal data

4. Measuring whether the extracted data conform to the delta between the beginning and ending balances in the system

Data Assimilation

For data to be processed consistently, they need to be assimilated into a comparative data structure. For example, a company may have multiple accounts-payable systems for a variety of acquired business divisions, but for purchasing power to be assessed, the combined vendor population across all systems needs to be aggregated for review. With combined data on all its vendors, the company can enter any subsequent vendor negotiations. Also, to provide a proper baseline for comparison, the data need to be robust. Such a baseline may be as simple as one additional year of data for establishing a business process benchmarking, or it can span to the robustness of a predictive model based on comparisons with multiple peer-company data sets.

Analytics Results

Too many data analysts are overconfident about their results. The level of testing to validate this confidence should be assessed in line with the value placed on the accuracy of the resulting insights for decision making. For example, a statement in structured query language (SQL) may be assumed to be accurate because it is in SQL. However, for making critical decisions—and aside from the usual testing completed by the user and programmer—it may be more effective to test the analytics techniques in a different programming language, such as Python, audit command language (ACL), or international data encryption language (IDEA), to ensure that parallel simulations lead to the same result.

Based on our experience, internal auditors are rarely involved in testing the code around the company's accounting system. But they could add significant value to this process. For example, one firm had auditors recalculate an accounts-payable report. The process, which took a minute or two using ACL software, saved the company tens of millions of dollars.[1] While the practice may not always result in such large returns, it's always worthwhile.

User Aptitude and Feedback

Ultimately, analytics provide actionable insights to businesspeople capable of under-standing the results. While complicated analytics models can be superior in some ways, they are useless if the end user can't comprehend the findings. Leaders often overlook the importance of training end users to interpret analytics and provide feedback to the team because these tasks are overshadowed by the focus on gener-ating reports. However, given that analytics can lead to a number of false positive (and negative) results, capable end users provide essential feedback in identifying new and improved methods for measuring analytics, such as better filters and calcu-lations. Tracking feedback can improve predictive and prescriptive analytics models; without such feedback, analytics become one-way communication with no way of assessing their effectiveness.

For every analytics use case, the quality of the output from each of the above steps should be measured and improvement plans set. Enhancements in the quality of data, execution, and user acceptance are likely to not only pay for themselves but also pay large dividends each time they are reviewed. For each deployed analytics method, a simple tracking of how users work with the tools could instill enthu-siasm across the entire organization, especially if any of the new approaches to data measurement result in cost savings or revenue increases.

Speed to Insights

Insights from data rarely emerge quickly. But in the fast-changing world of data, there is little time to waste. By optimizing each of the following elements, an orga-nization can work to keep pace with its ever-changing array of data.

Data Management

Mathematically speaking, the speed to making a decision based on analytics depends on how quickly data can be acquired, ingested, and analyzed. Much of the analytics process involves organizing data for analysis. Therefore, improvements in this area can have the biggest impact on expediting the decision-making process. Factors that might lead to these improvements include better understanding of the enterprise systems that provide the data, more efficient data assimilation, and learning from user feedback which data are most critical. The critical data required for company decision making should be carved out for analysis from the sea of the organization's big data, thereby expediting the delivery of analytics results.

Analytics Delivery

An organization's analytics capabilities tend to follow a maturity curve, from ad-hoc projects to continuous analysis. Generally speaking, analytics should start with a series of prototypes, which will tend to be ad hoc, and use many models that will be overwritten with improvements based on end-user feedback. Once the company has developed a model, it should implement an automated solution to provide a continuous stream of up-to-date results to the user. However, not all decision-making data needs to be run with such consistency; sometimes automation might not be worth the investment. A strategic choice might be to focus on those analytics that can be delivered in continuous, real-time fashion, such as external penetration monitoring of sensitive client data. In contrast, analyses that may require a month's worth of data to be useful—such as customer complaint trends—can run at irregular intervals and still be effective. The key is to focus on the strategic importance of the decision at hand and how the relevant information affects the decision.

Application Ease

In an optimal setting, users have on-demand access to the analytics they need for good decision making via a self-service application. Otherwise, a bottleneck is likely to form, with data unavailable for review until a specific program has been run by an analytics team. When possible, analytics, especially those that may be reviewed intermittently and without a structured schedule, should be available for teams to execute on demand. For example, a scoring analytic for determining a customer's level of credit should be available at the time of the sale to the customer. Otherwise, the customer may buy from a competitor even as credit management is waiting for approval from the system. Further, the level of documentation and training can be a determining factor in whether an end user assimilates the knowledge gained from the analysis or walks away without really understanding how to apply the information.

While quality is still paramount, it needs to be balanced with speed to ensure the organization's smooth operation. Quality findings delivered too late to influence decisions are worthless, and incomplete findings delivered quickly can do damage. The requirements for each analytics project should inform the right balance.

Return on Investment

In determining the success of an analytics project, most organizations ultimately focus on the most important measurement of all: the ROI of human capital, time, and cash. The quality and speed of analytics depend on how well the technology is operating. However, if the end result of a high-quality and expedient analytic provides no tangible return to the organization, leadership is likely to view the project as a failure (although the data scientist may see it as a valuable technology breakthrough). With a good cross-sectional knowledge of the business, internal audit is in a good position to calculate ROI independently and objectively. With this in mind, below are a variety of factors associated with measuring analytics ROI.

Improved Investments

For companies that are pursuing growth through mergers and acquisitions (M&A), analytics can assist with assessing the top risks and opportunities the acquiring company should focus on and informing post-merger decisions. As a simple and quality-related example, audit teams may spend days reviewing a variety of company reports in an attempt to identify journal entries that exhibit management override. To save time and improve the quality of the decisions about which entries to test, the audit team may decide to use a scoring model that runs 25 reports and ranks the potential acquisitions by their composite scores. This information could save the audit team days of reviewing false-positive journal entries in a number of reports.

Even more important, perhaps, the analytics team could look at all the hours spent on the audit, focusing the analytics on testing revenue and accounts receivable, which is where the majority of audit time is spent.

Productivity Improvements

Statistical sampling offers many benefits, including less time spent on reviews by a quality-review team—though the time reduction often leaves professionals wondering if they have missed a glaring error. Although a statistician could use dizzying mathematics to disprove a finding, the ability to analyze 100 percent of data when testing a control attribute can not only provide an efficient means of review but also may lead to no control exceptions that require testing. In this case, higher quality is coupled with enhanced productivity. CAEs must be aware of this potential and ready to pursue it. Additional returns on an analytics investment might be generated by analyzing data to assess the work effort at each stage of a process—thus identifying any bottlenecks and enabling more appropriate work assignments.

Professional Intelligence

One of the most difficult things to measure is how well end users—not the data scientist—are using data in their decision-making processes. Ultimate benefits should be calculated by counting the new decisions made by "field users," not by a centralized technology team. For example, a list of new business strategies or process improvements should be periodically updated in a tracking system. This measurement will indicate whether the organization is improving, how employee mind-sets are adjusting to a culture of data-driven decisions, and where the company is in relation to its peers in the industry.

Counting Cash Savings

The amount of cash savings is usually considered the best measure of an initiative's success. Easier availability of cash for payroll, just-in-time inventory purchase capabilities, and more timely payment collections from customers—all possible improvements with the help of analytics—not only impress senior management but also increase the likelihood of additional investments in analytics. While internal auditors have the skills to complete such an assessment, they rarely perform them, focusing their efforts instead on bolstering controls and other activities. But paying attention to cash savings can lead to big payoffs.

When prioritizing cash savings, the team should not necessarily focus on the area of largest expense, the area least frequently reviewed, or even the area suspected of harboring the most errors or fraud. Instead, it should focus on the area that will quickly yield a positive return on its analysis. Such a problem area may be travel spending, freight costs, overstated revenues, or vendor credit collection. For example, unless the enterprise is already doing regular accounts-payable recovery reviews, this is an area for possible cost savings, especially if the analysis is applied to the vendors with the highest recovery rates.

● ● ●

For companies that are piloting analytics projects, measurement is an essential way to determine effectiveness. Once analytics become embedded in the organization, calculating the impact of investments in analytics often falls by the wayside—either in the rush to fulfill requests from different business units or because of an assumption that simply using analytics represents progress. This framework to gauge ROI can help executives make strategic investments in analytics capabilities and ensure that they are achieving tangible results.

HOW TO APPLY ANALYTICS TO AN ENTERPRISEWIDE RISK ASSESSMENT

*"Sense and deal with problems in their smallest state,
before they grow bigger and become fatal."*

—Pearl Zhu

In a continually changing risk landscape, decision makers confront a wide range of uncertain outcomes. For many organizations, day-to-day operational decisions are fraught with uncertainty. Risk assessments are critical to helping organizations quickly identify and adapt to changes in the risks that most affect their businesses. In organizations with internal audit functions, the internal auditors typically perform an annual risk assessment as part of their effort to develop a risk-based internal audit plan. The objective of this assessment is to determine their overall audit strategy and tactics, mainly by looking at financial reporting controls and the output of the organization's overall enterprisewide risk assessment.

Many companies perform an assessment that is carried out outside of internal audit and meant to be a more expansive review, assessing internal and external risks across the entire organization. These assessments are often performed by a single function with risk-management responsibilities—for example, the general counsel, corporate compliance, treasury, or insurance department. These functions complete risk assessments by conducting interviews and sometimes surveys that are meant to help decision makers sort out priorities, set strategy, and define business objectives. When risk assessments are performed by just one segment or function of the business, however, the result can fail to integrate risk management with business objectives and company strategy—a failure to manage enterprise risk effectively. A truly enterprisewide risk assessment, on the other hand, can be used not only by internal audit but also by executive leadership and the board of directors to more effectively identify and prioritize risks, including new and emerging ones.

By embedding data analytics into risk assessments, organizations can gain greater visibility into critical risks in finance, compliance, operations, and, in some cases, strategy. Analytical tools that incorporate both qualitative and quantitative factors throughout an enterprise platform can help align the various functions in an organization, as well as help automate risk functions and controls testing. A well-functioning, overall risk-assessment process that integrates strategy and business objectives with risk and opportunity is critical to accelerate growth and improve performance.

Data-Driven, Enterprisewide Risk Assessment: An Overview

The *Enterprise Risk Management – Integrating with Strategy and Performance* framework developed by the Committee of Sponsoring Organizations of the Treadway Commission (COSO) defines enterprisewide risk management (ERM) as "the culture, capabilities, and practices, integrated with strategy and execution, that organizations rely on to manage risk in creating, preserving, and realizing value."[1] As COSO notes, "Integrating enterprise risk management practices throughout an organization improves decision-making in governance, strategy, objective-setting, and day-to-day operations. It helps to enhance performance by more closely linking strategy and business objectives to risk."

The best approach to enterprisewide risk assessment involves both a strategic (top-down) and operational (bottom-up) process to identify potential risks. The output—a prioritized risk register—can be mapped within the three lines of defense: frontline process owners, functions such as risk management that are responsible for oversight of controls, and the internal audit department, which audits the controls.

This is an oft-repeated refrain, but it is as true for risk assessment as for any other business function: it is not enough just to have an abundance of data. Decision makers must *understand* the data for the information to be useful. Analysts must work with those who own the business requirements to connect the dots—that is, to link data to the identification of risk and potential risk-mitigation strategies.

What Data Are Critical for a Companywide Risk Assessment?

The types of data that can be used to assess risk depend on the organization and its industry. All organizations, however, can begin by using financial information for key analytics and potential indicators. In this context, when determining the data to be used, CAEs can consider the overall risk environment, data access, and areas where they want to reduce detection risk and enhance continuous monitoring. The general ledger and supporting subledgers are among the most critical areas of focus for data-driven risk assessment. The focus here is transactional-level review, which should include several standard tests. First, transactional scoring of journal entries based on set criteria will isolate the entries that pose the highest risk, such as those containing unusual or incomplete descriptions. Also, it's wise to include areas that may be susceptible to fraud, such as cash, accounts payable, and accounts receivable. Reviewing monthly cash transactions could include a program of foreign entity review for violations of the Foreign Corrupt Practices Act (FCPA).[2]

In addition to ledgers, most organizations can tap their human resources departments for a number of key data points, such as the number of employees versus subcontractors, full time versus part time, employee turnover, retention rates, loss of key skill sets, and training programs in place. Along with transaction types and volumes, this information may help identify areas of risk such as understaffing or the need for training in handling certain types of transactions.

Finally, external information provides critical context for what's happening within the industry and beyond. These data points are crucial to the risk-assessment process because they provide early-warning signals of potential new risks. At no cost, many industry and trade organizations provide data on key trends as well as risk and performance indicators. They also may be able to provide an overall economic outlook for specific industries, sectors, and geographic locations in which they do business. Risk-management teams also must make a concerted effort to gather information on competitors to confirm the completeness of their risk universe. Further, organizations must implement processes to acquire critical customer information from their frontline employees. All these data will help identify any potential disruption in the industry as early as possible.

For one U.S. hedge fund, for example, analytics have become an increasingly important part of how the organization manages larger and larger amounts of data, reporting requirements, and staff changes all at once. The fund's CAE says that analytics help the fund isolate potential errors and fraudulent activity (namely, management exercising undue influence to change financial results) for additional testing. The firm also uses analytics as part of technology testing. It may quantify the types of changes made to applications—emergency, standard, or other, for example—to check for an overabundance of changes being made without going through the normal change control process. Internal audit can then have informed discussions with technology managers to determine the reasons for this pattern and recommend corrective actions.

As staff sizes shrink and outsourcing continues to grow, the fund uses analytics to reveal the areas in which those changes occurred. This detection helps to focus monitoring and continuous-auditing efforts on areas of higher change frequencies—in other words, where there is higher operational risk. Importantly, the CAE notes that analytics may provide useful and relevant information and point auditors in a certain direction. "However, it does not take the place of judgment and common sense."

Aligning All Three Lines of Defense

In our recent survey of some 150 CAEs, audit directors, and audit managers or supervisors, the majority (63 percent) agreed it would be useful to have an enterprise platform that could support analytics across the entire company. This finding was not surprising. Seventy-six percent of our survey respondents reported that they consolidate risk-assessment data manually across their organizations. They also reported that many diverse areas within their organizations work on risk management, including ERM specialists, internal auditors, internal control specialists, legal professionals, compliance officers, and individuals responsible for fraud and corruption.

In 2013, The IIA released a concept to help organizations more effectively coordinate their risk-management approach. The Three Lines of Defense model encompasses these functions:[3]

- The first line of defense is operational management, comprising frontline functions such as sales and customer service or procurement. These frontline process owners also own and manage risk, which entails designing and implementing operating control procedures on a day-to-day basis. They also are responsible for identifying and correcting control deficiencies.

- The second line of defense is risk-management and compliance functions that educate, train, and otherwise assist the first line. They monitor what the first line does, ensuring that controls are operating as designed. Such functions may include the risk-management department, the compliance department, and the controller's department that monitors financial reporting risk.

- The third line of defense is the internal audit department, which provides the audit committee and senior management with independent assurance of findings, processes, and controls.

When using analytics to strengthen risk management, it is vital to determine the best line of defense for each control to identify where that control should reside, who is responsible for it, and how to automate the test so it happens in real time. Usually this type of analytics is done at the transaction level so that a control deficiency or anomaly can be detected at the earliest possible point.

To succeed, these three lines of defense must be tightly coordinated and reflect business priorities. The best way to align the three lines of defense is for senior management—or a governing body such as the board of directors—to properly communicate the expectations for each line. Organizations should develop policies, document role definitions, and share these materials among groups to promote efficiency and effectiveness and avoid confusion of roles and responsibilities.

Performing an Analytics Risk Assessment

Developing an analytics risk assessment unfolds in the following four steps:

1. Determine what business areas and processes to include.
2. Identify risk levels or categories.
3. Name the data-driven factors of risk to be assessed.
4. Design analytics capabilities to measure and report increased levels of risk.

As previously noted, the ultimate goal is to link data to the identification of risk and potential risk-mitigation strategies. The result of this process should be a series of dashboards that decision makers can use to gain insights and detect emerging risks with enough time to take corrective action.

Step 1: Determine What to Include

Any data-driven risk-assessment process must begin by defining the areas and key business systems that will support the assessment process. To obtain actionable insights that will have a measurable effect on the business, companies should begin with their strategy and business objectives. What are the company's mission, vision, and values? What is the company seeking to achieve? Risks can then be identified based on the chosen strategy and business objectives. But as COSO points out, this is only one aspect to consider. Two additional factors can have far greater effect on an entity's value: the possibility that the company's strategy is not aligned with its mission, vision, and values; and the implications from the selected strategy. These questions should be explored to identify strategic risks where the stakes are highest. Other risks—such as operational, regulatory and compliance, or IT risks— also should be discussed to identify specific business problems and opportunities.

Risk-assessment leaders also must consider the external environment. Customers, suppliers, competitors, regulators, and others can have an influence on a company's strategy and business objectives. COSO notes several external factors "that can be categorized by the acronym PESTLE: political, economic, social, technological, legal, and environmental." Companies should approach each factor individually and analyze potential effects on their efforts.

Step 2: Identify Risk Levels or Categories

In Step 1, companies determined their internal and external risk categories. Now they must define their risk levels in terms of risk appetite and tolerance. How much risk is the company willing to take in pursuit of its mission, vision, strategy, and business objectives? This risk can be defined qualitatively or quantitatively. It may be defined broadly or more granularly according to the specific areas identified in Step 1. Either way, it should be articulated in terms of achieving a desired level of performance or outcome.

Risk levels then need to be defined. Two common measures are impact (or significance) and likelihood. Impact may be defined by the effect on the company's strategy, business objectives, brand and reputation, legal and regulatory actions, operations, and financials, among others. Likelihood may be defined by the possibility of a risk occurring—for example, from rare to almost certain, or other similar scales. The severity of risk levels can be based on a scale, such as one to five. It is important to measure severity, as it is a critical input to decision making on risk response. Severity levels are generally determined after considering the company's risk preparedness—which may include the policies, procedures, and controls in place or soon to be implemented that will alter the risk severity.

Step 3: Name the Data-Driven Factors of Risk to Be Assessed

One of the top challenges to incorporating analytics into the risk-assessment process is identifying and obtaining sources of data. Traditionally, the process has been manual, time intensive, limited to a small portion of a company's data environment, reactive, and not standardized. The future state is automated, proactive, and fast. It takes place in real time and includes all data for thorough evaluation.

Following are the key steps in the process:

1. Agree on critical questions and identify information sources, file attributes, and record layouts. Then determine how they will be used.

2. Collect and assemble data.

3. Assess the data quality.

4. Integrate multisource and multistructured data entered into an analytics tool.

5. Determine what reports and insights would be most helpful for decision makers.

6. Share results in an understandable way, making sure that there's a clear path to operationalization.

Step 4: Design Your Analytics Capabilities

Last, companies will need to design their capabilities. This task begins with the selection of technology tools based on the set of objectives the company is trying to meet through the risk-assessment process. Companies now have access to a wide range of tools, and every organization's decision criteria will be unique. Some factors that may affect decisions are the organization's specific data sources, formats, transaction volume, and reporting requirements. For example, some tools are better than others at the visualizations of trends. Good visual programs apply a variety of statistical techniques to create charts that help risk managers to detect outliers and suspicious transactions and trends in general ledger volume. Digital analysis can examine year-over-year variances and evaluate values versus volumes.

These are just some of the analytics that can be applied to the general ledger in order to identify and assess risk.

An Effective Approach to Continuous Risk Assessment and Monitoring

A continuous-monitoring approach should include all processes that management puts in place to ensure that all policies and procedures are operating effectively. In the survey mentioned above, 49 percent of respondents acknowledged that their companies' current processes can take weeks, months, or even quarters to respond to control failures and risks (see exhibit 7-1). Further, 40 percent said that their organizations perform neither continuous monitoring nor continuous auditing. Use of continuous-monitoring procedures assures management that controls are operating effectively and that the information being produced is both relevant and reliable—and it can help the organization control failures and risks more efficiently.

Continuous-monitoring techniques may be expanded to other types of continual risk assessment and monitoring. A change in the dollar value of certain transactions, an increase or decrease in the number of customers, and the aging of receivables are just a few examples of how continuous monitoring can help risk assessment.

Exhibit 7-1: Few Companies Respond to Control Failures and Risks in Real Time

Only 5% respond to control failures in real time
The rest respond slowly in addressing control failures:

- Days — 45%
- Weeks — 24%
- Months — 19%
- Quarter or longer — 7%

Source: Grant Thornton

The U.S. hedge fund in the example above, for instance, performs continuous digital analysis on its disbursements. The theorem suggests that in a large population, beginning numbers (the first one or two digits) follow a certain frequency. After applying the theorem to the data, they look at the outliers. Recently, they found that in one six-month period, for example, the number "2" was the first digit on disbursements with a frequency significantly higher than expected. Returning to the data, the fund selected a larger sample of disbursements to review and verified that there was no fraudulent activity. Similarly, the fund analyzes the number of payments and amounts paid to specific vendors. This review reveals whether one vendor is favored over another to the detriment of the firm, as well as whether the firm is taking advantage of all available discounts.

Such automated tests are essential in helping management continue to identify risks and develop ways to mitigate those risks on an ongoing basis.

Implementing Automated Testing of the Most Critical Enterprise Risks and Controls

Once the enterprise risk assessment is complete, organizations must identify the most efficient and effective way to test these risks and controls. The focus should be on the highest risk areas and on areas where automated testing will be most beneficial. Automation can provide substantial savings in labor and reduce overall detection risk—that is, the risk that a process will conclude that there are no errors in a population when in fact there are. Moreover, automation can drastically reduce or even eliminate detection risk by allowing organizations to analyze larger samples—in some cases, entire populations—to identify all exceptions. The following areas can be especially conducive to automated testing.

Compliance

In most organizations, compliance is ready for automation, which can detect and correct errors or anomalies in transactional data early on. Continuous-monitoring programs also are excellent candidates, as real-time transactional review can be greatly beneficial for compliance efforts.

Accounts Payable

For many companies, expenditures are a high-priority area for risk management because the outlay of cash has greater potential for fraud. This area can be reviewed for control deficiencies, anomalies in the data, and evidence of malfeasance. Accounts payable also can be assessed for trends related to performance and overall efficiencies that can reduce the cost to process a transaction or identify potential product deficiencies.

The associated first lines of defense may choose to review controls for duplicate payments to vendors, ensuring that the same individuals who initiate purchase orders (POs) are *not* the ones who approve them; three-way matching of invoices; matching POs and bills of lading to the vendor master file; and proper application controls to assure proper input, processing, and output controls.

For example, a national airline wished to identify which areas within their accounting process should be analyzed to identify and subsequently mitigate risk. By profiling the company's accounts-payable procedures and associated data points, team members identified transactions with a high likelihood for duplicate payments and overpayments. Using a combination of analytics tools, they applied a risk model to prioritize which vendors and specific transactions were candidates for these duplicate payments and overpayments. They contacted the high-risk vendors to obtain confirmation against the airline's data and worked to collect the unrecognized credits.

As a result of the analysis, the airline was able to recover more than $1.5 million. The process also uncovered several root causes and enhancement opportunities that the airline has incorporated into its accounts-payable process. Based on the success of this effort, the airline intends to apply data analytics beyond the accounting and finance function in its fuel-management, inventory, and even revenue-enhancement operations.

A Phased Approach to an Accounts-Payable Risk Assessment

This simple, three-step approach can help companies avoid duplicating payments or overpaying vendors, leading to significant cost savings over time.

Phase 1: Model the risks and prioritize which vendors and transactions to assess.

Phase 2: Perform a vendor confirmation and identify the credit due to the client. Collect the credit or apply it to future invoices.

Phase 3: Implement a continuous-monitoring system in the accounts-payable process.

Data analytics can be used to address enterprise risk in accounts payable related to control, quality, cost, and performance risks. These efforts may include defining performance measures around labor cost and accounts-payable performance, quality-based performance measures regarding errors in the processing of invoices, or the canceling or returning of a product due to poor performance. Also, analysts might include time-based measures on the efficiency of the process or the number of days to pay and invoice, which could indicate potential credit risks or the inability to follow up on outstanding invoices.

● ● ●

The benefits of an analytics approach to risk assessments are clear: companies can quickly identify and quantify higher areas of risk, continually monitor key risks, detect data anomalies and trends, and efficiently analyze large populations of data. The use of analytics during the risk-assessment process increases the chances that companies can uncover their most important risks, therefore assuring that they are spending their time and resources in the right areas.

CONCLUSION

The recent evolution of data and analytics provides companies with limitless opportunities to capture more value. At this point, most organizations know they need to implement analytics in their operations, but many struggle with how best to do that. Charging blindly ahead—without a clear direction or an understanding of the goals of an analytics program—will result in suboptimal results.

As a company moves down the path to implementing analytics, the material in this book will help managers and decision makers gain the necessary perspective to develop a strategy or hone existing efforts—even as continued innovation and technological advances are creating new applications for technologies.

It falls on executives to understand the stakes and the path forward—they will be the ones to strike the optimal balance between humans and machines and unlock the full potential of analytics in their organization. And to do so, they must first have the capabilities, processes, and talent to aggregate the data necessary to solve their business problems. Then they can think about prioritizing a digital transformation, formulating use cases, blending data, measuring the impact of analytics, and harnessing analytics in risk.

Companies must understand not only where their data resides and how to aggregate it but also how to combine different data sets in order to uncover patterns and insights that might otherwise be hidden. They must learn to focus only on those opportunities with the most promise—and the biggest potential to create value. They must ensure they are getting the insights they set out to find and assess efforts in terms of time, cost, and quality. And they must identify their most important risks and assure that they are spending their time and resources in the right areas.

It's a lot to consider. But with a united effort and structured approach, companies will be well on their way to truly changing the way their organization does business and how they conceptualize success and growth. They will gain insights they never thought possible thanks to a transparent, cohesive, and efficient organization.

NOTES

Chapter 1
The Keys to Analytics Success

1. Alex Q. Arbuckle, "1996–1997: The Kasparov-Deep Blue chess matches," Mashable, February 10, 2016, mashable.com; Darrell Etherington, "Google's AlphaGo AI beats the world's best human Go player," TechCrunch, May 23, 2017, techcrunch.com.

2. In partnership with The IIA's Internal Audit Foundation and Audit Executive Center, Grant Thornton conducted a series of surveys on analytics in early 2017. The sample included nearly 170 chief audit executives, audit directors, and audit managers or supervisors across a range of company sizes and industries.

3. Ibid.

4. Ibid.

5. "The need to lead in data and analytics," McKinsey & Company, April 2016, mckinsey.com.

6. Grant Thornton survey in partnership with The IIA's Internal Audit Foundation and the Audit Executive Center.

Chapter 2
The Changing Data and Analytics Needs of Companies

1. Grant Thornton survey in partnership with The IIA's Internal Audit Foundation and the Audit Executive Center.

2. For a more detailed discussion of the types of analytics, see Warren W. Stippich, Jr. and Bradley J. Preber, *Data Analytics: Elevating Internal Audit's Value*, Grant Thornton and the Internal Audit Foundation (Lake Mary, FL: Internal Audit Foundation, 2016).

3. Helen Mayhew, Tamim Saleh, and Simon Williams, "Making data analytics work for you—instead of the other way around," *McKinsey Quarterly*, October 2016, mckinsey.com.

Chapter 3
A Digital Transformation to Unlock Analytics

1. Information gathered through interviews.

2. Ibid.

Chapter 5
Detecting Trends and Patterns Through Blended Data

1. For more detail, see Karen A. Frenkel, "12 steps for analyzing unstructured data," *CIO Insight*, February 2, 2015, cioinsight.com.

Chapter 6
How to Measure the Value of Analytics

1. Rich Lanza, "My Best Money-Saving Audit Finding Ever," ACL, July 11, 2013, acl.com.

Chapter 7
How to Apply Analytics to an Enterprisewide Risk Assessment

1. Robert Hirth, *Enterprise Risk Management—Aligning Risk with Strategy and Performance*, Association for Federal Enterprise Risk Management, June 2016, aferm.org.

2. For more on the Foreign Corrupt Practices Act, visit justice.gov.

3. The IIA Position Paper "The Three Lines of Defense in Effective Risk Management and Control," The IIA, January 2013, na.theiia.org.

GLOSSARY OF TERMS

Analytics/data analytics: the computational analysis of data or statistics, often using algorithms or models to test specific hypotheses

Artificial intelligence: the development of computer systems able to perform tasks that normally require human intelligence

Blended data: formed by combining different data sources into a consolidated data set, enabling analysts to uncover patterns and exceptions that wouldn't be visible in individual data sets

Center of excellence (CoE): a central analytics function that supports the organization

Descriptive analytics: used to report and characterize past events by condensing large chunks of data into smaller, more meaningful bits of information

Design thinking: a methodology that draws upon logic, imagination, and intuition to explore possibilities of "what could be" as well as the associated benefits to the company, business unit, and end user or customer

Diagnostic analytics: provides insight into why certain trends or specific incidents occurred

Digitization: the process of converting documents and other assets into a digital format that can be stored and analyzed by computers

Machine learning: an application of artificial intelligence that provides systems with the ability to automatically learn and improve from experience without being explicitly programmed

Minimum viable product (MVP): the most basic solution and target operating model that can provide the defined capability and allow the organization to begin to capture value

Predictive analytics: allows users to identify trends and forecast future outcomes

Prescriptive analytics: uses a significant volume of data to link predictions to actions that will produce the best result

Sponsorship: championing an analytics initiative, providing direction and strategy, and ensuring the sufficient allocation of resources

Structured data: exists in an understandable, organized format that allows the data to be fed into a relational database management system for analysis, e.g., transactional data, customer data, and financial data

Text analytics: uses tools such as text mining, natural data processing, and analytics to identify patterns in unstructured data

Unstructured data: has no predefined organization format and is typically in a free-form, text-heavy format that makes in-depth analysis difficult, e.g., call center communications, open text fields, contract, and audio and video

INTERNAL AUDIT FOUNDATION SPONSORSHIP RECOGNITION

STRATEGIC PARTNERS

FOUNDATION PARTNERS

DIAMOND PARTNERS (US $25,000+)

Larry Harrington
CIA, QIAL, CRMA

PLATINUM PARTNERS (US $15,000-$24,999)

GOLD PARTNERS (US $5,000–$14,999)

**The Estate of
Wayne G. Moore**
CIA

97

MEMBERS

Kevin L. Cantrell, CIA,
Plains All American Pipeline

Brian P. Christensen, *Protiviti Inc.*

Jean Coroller, *The French
Institute of Directors*

Philip E. Flora, CIA, CCSA, *FloBiz
& Associates, LLC*

Stephen D. Goepfert, CIA,
CRMA, QIAL

Ulrich Hahn, CIA, CCSA,
CGAP, CRMA

Lisa Hartkopf, *Ernst & Young LLP*

Steven E. Jameson, CIA, CCSA,
CFSA, CRMA, *Community
Trust Bank*

Pamela Short Jenkins, CIA, CRMA,
Fossil, Inc.

Tow Toon Lim, CRMA,
DSO National Laboratories

James A. Molzahn, CIA, CRMA,
Sedgwick, Inc.

Frank M. O'Brien, CIA, QIAL, *Olin
Corporation*

Sakiko Sakai, CIA, CCSA, CFSA,
CRMA, *Infinity Consulting*

Tania Stegemann, CIA, CCSA,
CRMA, *CIMIC Group Limited*

Anton Van Wyk, CIA, CRMA, QIAL,
PricewaterhouseCoopers LLP

Yi Hsin Wang, CIA, CGAP, CRMA,
National Taipei University

Ana Cristina Zambrano Preciado,
CIA, CCSA, CRMA, *IIA–Colombia*

99

Stephen G. Goodson, CIA, CCSA, CGAP, CRMA, *UT Austin McCombs School*

Judy Grobler, CIA, CRMA

Kivilcim Gunbatti, *Ziraat Bank*

Yulia Gurman, CIA, *Packaging Corporation of America*

Beatrice Ki-Zerbo, CIA

Brian Daniel Lay, CRMA, *Ernst & Young LLP*

Steve Mar, CFSA

Jozua Francois Martins, CIA, CRMA, *Citizens Property Insurance Corporation*

Mani Massoomi, CFSA, CRMA, *TIAA*

Joseph A. Mauriello, CIA, CFSA, CRMA, *University of Texas at Dallas*

John D. McLaughlin, *The Audit Exchange LLC*

Mark J. Pearson, CIA

Jason Philibert, CIA, CRMA

Sundaresan Rajeswar, CIA, CCSA, CFSA, CGAP, CRMA, *Teyseer Group of Companies*

James M. Reinhard, CIA, *Simon Property Group*

Bismark Rodriguez, CIA, CCSA, CFSA, CRMA, *Financial Services Risk Management*

Hesham K. Shawa, *IIA Jordon – International*

Deanna F. Sullivan, CIA, CRMA, *SullivanSolutions*

Jason Robert Thogmartin, CIA, CRMA, *First Data Corporation*

Adriana Beatriz Toscano Rodriguez, CIA, CRMA, *UTE*

Jane Traub, CCSA, *The Nielsen Company*

Maritza Villanueva, CIA, *Regal Forest Holding*

Paul L. Walker, *St. John's University*

Larry G. Wallis, CIA, *VIA Metropolitan Transit*

Chance R. Watson, CIA, CRMA, *Texas Department of Family & Protective Services*

Klaas J. Westerling, CIA, *Intertrust Group Holding S.A.*